HOW TO PROVIDE OUTSTANDING SERVICE TO HOTELS
7 Ways to WOW Your Client

Zak Kogan

How to Provide Outstanding Service to Hotels: 7 Ways to WOW Your Clients
GoGreenOrganicCleaners.com

Copyright © 2020 Zak Kogan

ISBN: 979-8580176031

All rights reserved. No portion of this book may be reproduced mechanically, electronically, or by any other means, including photocopying, without permission of the publisher or author except in the case of brief quotations embodied in critical articles and reviews. It is illegal to copy this book, post it to a website, or distribute it by any other means without permission from the publisher or author.

References to internet websites (URLs) were accurate at the time of writing. Authors and the publishers are not responsible for URLs that may have expired or changed since the manuscript was prepared.

Limits of Liability and Disclaimer of Warranty
The author and publisher shall not be liable for your misuse of the enclosed material. This book is strictly for informational and educational purposes only.

Warning – Disclaimer
The purpose of this book is to educate and entertain. The author and/or publisher do not guarantee that anyone following these techniques, suggestions, tips, ideas, or strategies will become successful. The author and/or publisher shall have neither liability nor responsibility to anyone with respect to any loss or damage caused, or alleged to be caused, directly or indirectly by the information contained in this book.

Publisher
10-10-10 Publishing
Markham, ON Canada

Printed in the United States of America

Table of Contents

Acknowledgements vii
Foreword ix

Chapter 1 – From Physicist and Programmer to Servicing Hotels 1
How I Got into the Clothing Business 2
Why Hotels? 3
What Does This Have to do With My Trade? 5

Chapter 2 – What's in It for You? 9
Employees That Look the Part 11
The Challenges of a Dry-Cleaning Service 12

Chapter 3 – Position Yourself as a Problem Solver 17
Building a Successful System 17
The Value Vendors Can Bring 19

Chapter 4 – How My System to Service Hotels Was Created 23
Dry-Cleaning Becomes My Industry 24
Building a System With Quality in Mind 25

Chapter 5 – How to Train Your Employees 29
Shaping and Defining Your Team 30
Never Assume You Can't Improve 32
Redundancy is Key 33
Celebrating the Successes 35
Know the Members of Your Team 38

Chapter 6 – How to Train Hotel Employees 43
Implementing the System in Your Hotel 43
Accommodating the Needs of the Hotel Administration 45

Chapter 7 – How to Create One-Team Hotel Dry-Cleaning 49
The Critical Path: The Manual Binder 50
Key to Success: Communication 53

Chapter 8 – Conclusion 57

Bonus Section 61
Interview: Mark Giangiulio, General Manager of Grand Summit Hotel 63
Interview: Scott McArthur, General Manager of Madison Hotel 69
Interview: Lee Trilling, General Manager of Westin Hotel 77
Interview: Kevin Catrambon, General Manager of Hilton Garden Inn 85
Interview: Keith Moses, General Manager of Hilton Complex 91
Interview: Jim Hecox, General Manager of a Best Western 97
Interview: Paul Dolce, General Manager of Dolce Hotel 101

Testimonials 107
About the Author 109

I dedicate this book to all entrepreneurs who have the courage not to stop at the obstacles, but to continue to improve their businesses to get outstanding results in their lives and businesses.

Acknowledgements

Thank you to the following individuals, without whose help, this book, as well as my success, wouldn't be possible: Adam Markel, CEO of New Picks, and his staff of trainers and coaches, who helped me to get ideas on how to improve my business and my life; the general managers of different hotels, who helped me to understand the hotel business, especially Kevin Catrambone, Rany Baroudi, and David Ruas; my employees, who helped to design my system, and whose hard work brings outstanding results; my brother, Leonid, who was my partner in several of my businesses; and a special thanks to my family for their unconditional love and support.

Foreword

When you own a hospitality business, it is critical to offer an amazing experience for your clients every single time they interact with your team. For hotels, that amazing experience includes the various amenities being offered to your guests. *How to Provide Outstanding Service to Hotels: 7 Ways to WOW Your Client* is the guide to adding value for your guests by focusing on a simple service that can be seamlessly integrated into your hotel's offerings.

Zak Kogan spells out how he built his business around providing a key amenity to hotels through dry-cleaning. From the early stages of his journey to build his business, and illustrating how he connects with his hotel clients, Zak gives you the tools and skills necessary to create that same WOW experience for your guests.

How to Provide Outstanding Service to Hotels also shares how these value-added services can be integrated into your hotel. Zak offers his own training plan as a model for how to get employees on board and give them the tools to provide a WOW experience for every guest. Part of his journey was seeing himself as a problem-solver for his clients, giving them solutions and helping them to meet a variety of challenges.

Zak also shares how he celebrated the successes, inspiring his team to continue providing a WOW experience for his hotel clients and their guests. No matter what industry you are in, *How to Provide Outstanding Service to Hotels: 7 Ways to WOW Your Client* can guide you with a variety of tools to create a WOW experiences for your clients.

Raymond Aaron
New York Times Bestselling Author

Chapter 1

From Physicist and Programmer to Servicing Hotels

A weary traveler comes to a hotel looking for a place to rest and prepare for the next day's travel, or to enjoy a relaxing day at the pool. Quality hotels provide the clean room and quality service, but in today's world of social media and connectivity, that isn't enough. Sites that allow individuals to put their home up for rent, or offer rooms for reduced rates, have increased the competition the hotel industry faces. Now, more than ever, it is key for a hotel to offer something more that makes them stand out, from not only other hotels but even those sites with alternative options.

What can you offer to your guests? When you first look at your hotel, you might see the quality service that you are already providing. The rooms are clean, your staff is friendly and helpful, plus you offer some of what are now standard amenities, including a pool and exercise room. What more can we possibly do to compete?

The truth is that hotels compete best by offering convenience to their guests. What are some areas in which you can offer that convenience? One way is through dry-cleaning. It offers a simple way for guests to have a fresh outfit without trying to deal with the logistics of finding a dry cleaner or laundry, in a city where they aren't familiar with basic landmarks.

However, putting a system in place can be difficult, because you are dealing with a vendor outside of your company. Your reputation is totally tied into a service that is out of your control, because your guest associates any services with your hotel, not that vendor. The result is that you struggle to provide excellent service, but with little leverage in the execution.

When you look around your hotel, however, you are able to provide a variety of services that add value for your guests. How do you do so? Using various systems, your hotel runs like a well-oiled machine. Dry-cleaning, however, brings its own challenges. Here are just a few of them:

- Returning the right clothes in a timely fashion
- Addressing complaints and concerns effectively
- Completing a quality cleaning process in a short period
- Providing guest satisfaction every time

It was these issues that led me to create my system, allowing any hotel to implement it and offer quality and value to their guests. But what led me to the world of hotels? It started in college, with a bet.

How I Got into the Clothing Business

In the 1970s, I was in college, studying to be a physicist. This was a time of social change and the emergence of the hippy lifestyle. Of course, that meant plenty of spirited discussions about what men and women could do. My ego wouldn't let me acknowledge that there was something that I couldn't do as a man. During one of those talks, I told my girlfriend that as a man, I could do a better job than a woman, regardless the task. I threw in the traditional women's work, such as cleaning, cooking, and even tailoring. My girlfriend decided to make me put my money where my mouth is. She dared me to do some tailoring by making a garment. What I made was up to me. I was in trouble. She knew I couldn't even put a button on my shirt, let alone create a new piece of clothing from scratch.

However, I didn't back away from the challenge. I decided to make a shirt that had a zipper in front, mimicking a shirt I had seen on a band member that I liked. I thought I would do better if I was making something that I would like to wear. I bought a piece of bright yellow material, put it on the table, and started to cut. If any of you know how to sew, you can see that I might have been putting myself into a bad position. Before I got very far, I decided to use one of my own shirts as a pattern. Then, just to make sure it was big enough, I left an extra inch all around where I was cutting. I manually put all the pieces together, and the shirt I ended up with was almost twice as big as I needed. That extra inch had translated into a much larger shirt.

Another two weeks of work, and trial and error, finally left me with a shirt that I could wear. Our dormitory on the campus had a housekeeping room with an old, broken, manual sewing machine. My determination to succeed meant that I took the old machine apart and got it working again. Imagine the look on my girlfriend's face when I showed up to the discotheque, wearing a new handmade shirt. My roommates were jealous, and I won the bet. But there was another side effect from that experience. I found out that I really enjoyed sewing!

I decided to make matching pants, then a red jacket with silver buttons. The next 3 months, I didn't even study, because I was tailoring 12–16 hours a day, virtually non-stop! I believe my Jewish tailor ancestors were talking to my soul. It was no surprise then that when it was exam time, I was struggling. I failed one class, then another—one more and I would have been kicked out of college. I buckled down and studied with determination, and was able to pass my exams and stay in school. But that passion for tailoring was not extinguished. In fact, I became the tailor around the campus.

Why Hotels?

Over the years, I continued to sew, but I also finished school, becoming a physicist and a programmer. In the meantime, it meant I spent time traveling. Using dry-cleaning and tailoring services at various hotels was hit and miss. Sometimes the service was great, but other times, I didn't get my clothes back on time or I got things that weren't mine. I couldn't help but think that there must be a better way. There were systems for other aspects of the hotel, but it seemed as if dry-cleaning got left behind.

It became my goal to find a way to create a system that could be implemented, regardless of the hotel, to provide a valuable service to their guests. The reality is that hotels are income driven. They want to provide services to their guests that will get them to return and book a room in the hotel again. At the same time, they want to make sure that they keep reliable vendors working with them. This means that hotels are more likely to pay their bills on a timely basis. Plus, a hotel will typically have a set amount of guests they anticipate on a weekly basis. By working with the hotel, you can soon find the pattern in terms of how much work comes in on a weekly basis, how busy any particular day may be, or even how busy a particular season may be. Hotels will also want to make their vendors aware of the events occurring. If you provide excellent service and a quality product, then you will have steady income from that hotel for a long period of time.

Additionally, hotel managers are a relatively small group. One is likely to recommend a vendor that they have had success with, to others, thus increasing your business and increasing your income. If you provide excellent service and a good product or service, you can have steady income for a long time. However, it is important to remember that this is a service industry. One bad experience and you might lose a hotel client for good. Therefore, it isn't enough to just perform a decent service. You need to provide excellent service every time. As I will discuss later, that means not reaching one level and assuming that you can't improve.

When I think about any type of business, I think of the type of systems that can be put into place. Every time I do something that I may have to do again in the future, I look for the system that can be implemented, to make that repeat action easier the next time. When an action is not performed according to a system, it is much easier for mistakes to happen. How many times have you gone to a hotel and had issues with missing clothes, or a food order that was missing an item? The point is that each hotel employee might do things a little differently, which means a different result every time—not a good idea, especially in a service industry where guests demand excellence every time.

Many hotels have done their best to create systems to address multiple aspects of their business, but each one does things a little differently. When you go to a Sheraton hotel, the system is a Sheraton system. The next night, you might be staying at a Hilton, where they use the Hilton system. Each of these hotels can provide excellent service, as long as they follow their systems, and the employees do things the same way every time. Yet when it comes to vendors, particularly those who handle dry-cleaning, there is no system, and the results are rarely as excellent as the guest hopes. We assist hotels to create a proven system that allows them to provide outstanding service to their guests in this area, making them number one in their industry.

What Does This Have to do With My Trade?

Creating this system involved tapping into my experiences outside of the hotel industry. I was trained to develop systems, and my love of sewing and tailoring meant that I took my expertise to the clothing industry. When it comes to creating clothing, systems are key so that you have a quality product for your customers. Without the right systems, the product is not produced consistently. No matter who I worked for, the idea was always the same. I was looking for the repetitive actions that I could build a system around. Yet most of these systems were contained within one company, and the number of moving parts was limited.

As I mentioned earlier, changes in my professional industry gave me the opportunity to expand out from the clothing industry into the hotel industry. When I talked with various members of the hotel industry about developing a dry-cleaning system, many of them said that it couldn't be done. These were 20 and 30-year veterans of the hotel industry. In their minds, the number of moving parts, plus the fact that each hotel has their own systems already in place, made the idea of creating a system that would work in any hotel just too difficult.

The reality is that while each hotel has their own way of doing things, so does each dry-cleaning vendor. It is an industry with its own culture and way of doing business. As you will see, I found a way to combine these various moving parts to create a system that can be implemented into any hotel, and successfully provide a value-added service for your guests.

Yet in the early stages of developing my system, I learned that even the best system can have areas that need to improve. In my case, I had this brought home to me in the form of a mixed-up shirt that traveled from one hotel to another. This particular hotel manager had traveled and stayed in one of the other hotels in his chain that also used my service. Along the way, he grabbed one of their dry-cleaning bags. Now each hotel that works with me has bags that are specifically tagged for their hotel. This helps us as part of the tracking process.

When this manager got back to their hotel, they gathered a few items for dry-cleaning and sent them in with that day's pickup. The next day, however, the shirt and other items had not made it back to the hotel. After extensive searching and tracking, we finally found the items at the hotel where the manager had stayed the night before. What happened? The hotel manager had used the wrong hotel bag, and so their items had been sent, not to their hotel but to another hotel within the chain.

However, because of the way my system is designed, we were able to find those missing items, even though they were across town at a different hotel. In this case, the mistake happened through a mix-up by the manager, but if your system can't adapt for human error, then it will be impossible to provide that outstanding and excellent service to your guests every time.

At other times, however, the guests themselves will provide the challenge. In this particular case, we had an entire rugby team stay at one of the hotels that I take care of. There were a variety of clothes that needed to be cleaned for each member of the team, including jerseys and team uniforms. The challenge didn't end in just the large volume of clothes that needed to be cleaned and pressed, but the team manager had experience with items coming up missing or being given to the wrong team member. As a result, he had created his own system to make sure that everyone got back their items. His experience had not been one of outstanding service up to that point. Now, my system could have easily taken care of their large order and gotten everyone back their items, but in order to make the manager feel at ease, I accommodated his system into ours. While it did require more work, he was satisfied, and all the effort meant that we had a very happy guest.

One of the things I have learned over the years is that making the guest happy means that you need to be flexible. The same is true if you are a vendor for various hotels. You need to be available and flexible to accommodate their needs. At the same time, I have learned that you have to be realistic in managing your clients' expectations. While we always do our best to make sure that we turn orders around the same day, we still need at least 4 hours to complete the job properly and to make sure the clothes look their best. Working with a new hotel, I outline our pickup and delivery times, because I want to make sure they understand that some deadlines are fixed. That being said, I always do my best to accommodate my clients, and they have rewarded me with even more business.

Part of the system depends on the hotel. When they do not follow it, problems can result. In the next few chapters, I will be talking about my system in greater detail, but I will also be talking about training that is key for the hotel staff as well. In one instance, a hotel employee, who had not been trained on the system, took a dry-cleaning bag from a guest, but it did not get delivered to the right area for pickup. Thus, the guests were looking for their clothes the next day, and they had not been cleaned. The hotel eventually found the bag, and we made that order a top priority to satisfy the guest and my client. Even though the error was not mine, I made adjustments because I wanted to provide outstanding service. The hotel manager was grateful, and I was able to go to the hotel and do some necessary retraining to avoid these issues in the future.

Many hotels recognize that there are benefits to providing these additional services for their guests, but they also recognize that there are a lot of potential problems that can result. If they have had a bad experience with their vendors in the past, it can be difficult to trust a new vendor that claims they can provide outstanding service consistently. In my case, I was offering a new system that was unlike anything most hotel managers had ever seen.

When I first started out, I didn't have a portfolio of happy clients to show to hotels. I just had a system and a plan to provide outstanding service to these hotels. Using my contacts in the clothing industry, I was able to make a connection with my first hotel. I remember offering them the opportunity to test drive my system. As I have mentioned repeatedly, hotels have issues with their vendors on a regular basis. I pointed out that they wouldn't settle for sub-par service from other vendors, yet they do from their dry-cleaning vendor. It was that tactic and my faith in my system that got me in the door. Today, my system is in multiple hotels. Additionally, I have created a system that can easily be adapted to hotels across the country.

How to Provide Outstanding Service to Hotels

As you will see in the next chapter, there are multiple benefits for you as the hotel manager, including providing excellent service over and over again for your guests. As we all know, a happy guest is likely to recommend your hotel, but also likely to be a repeat guest!

Chapter 2

What's in It for You?

As a hotel, the reality is that you are always trying to keep up with the Joneses, so to speak. Many hotels are updating to reflect the connectivity that guests require to work, play, and socialize. This means upgrading internet access and providing consistent high-speed Wi-Fi. But the expectations of guests have continued to go up. What was once considered exceptional service is now considered standard, and guests have come to expect it with every room, every time.

Often, adding a service is not necessarily as much about making your hotel stand out from the crowd as it is about keeping up with the crowd. You don't want to be skipped by a potential guest just because you don't offer the same amenities as the hotel down the street. With the various review and hotel booking sites available, it is easier than ever for a guest to see if your amenities match the hotel down the street. Value isn't just about the price, but what you offer as part of that room price.

Business travelers provide a different challenge, because they aren't often in town to enjoy the local attractions and explore your community. They are there for a specific purpose, which means they need a business center that can accommodate their needs for printing and faxing. Reliable internet connections are also a necessity. When providing internet as an amenity, have you struggled with the provider to make sure your guests are satisfied? How many times do you allow the provider to not provide quality service before you cut that contract? Their performance reflects on you, and you aren't willing to risk your reputation with a type of guest that may end up visiting your hotel multiple times throughout the year, often telling other associates about their experience. Those recommendations are key to future and repeat business.

As hotel managers, you are always evaluating your service and grading your own paper. Those online reviews also provide a way for you to identify weaknesses and strengths. Your staff depend on your direction and leadership to provide the best guest experience possible. Without it, the consistency that draws your guests back will be lacking. Keeping a customer costs much less than attracting a new one. When it comes to business traveling guests, attracting and keeping them means meeting their expectations at every stay.

Business travelers, in particular, use certain services that your other guests might not need. But if they are using a dry-cleaning service from your hotel, then they are expecting exceptional service. Timing is critical for them. They may only travel with a couple of key outfits, so they need everything back on time and in good order. But you are depending on an outside vendor to complete this process effectively. Still, if it doesn't happen right, then your staff are the ones who will have to handle the irate guest.

When there are problems, how do you handle it? Training staff to handle guest complaints is important for meeting their expectations. It isn't easy to anticipate every need of your guests, and mistakes do happen. It is important, therefore, to empower staff by training them on how to effectively deal with a guest who is not happy. But how can your staff deal with a problem that originates outside of your system?

The answer is to find a vendor that not only provides a service, but also brings a system that can assist your hotel in effectively delivering services to their guests. This system needs to easily adapt to your hotel's processes, and be simple to integrate. Otherwise, it creates a burden that can outweigh the benefits of the system to your hotel and your guests. When you do find the vendor that fits, you are able to upsell your guests in terms of the services that they use at your hotel. You are offering convenience and anticipating their needs. It is the type of service business travelers remember, and they frequently come back.

Do you have conventions or trade shows that frequently come into your area? Are your rooms full, or do you find that you aren't commanding the larger share of the business that you could have? If your rooms aren't full, then you are losing market share. We all know that market share is key to driving your revenue numbers up and meeting your goals in terms of sales for the week, the month, the quarter, and the year. If your hotel is part of a chain system, then you also have to meet the revenue expectations of the chain and your bosses further up the ladder. The question is, how can you leverage your vendors to create the experiences that will have your guests coming back and telling others?

Here's where my system comes into play. It offers not only the added service of same day dry-cleaning, but it also is a system that can be integrated easily into your hotel. My system can be adapted to meet other needs, providing a blueprint of how to adapt other outside vendors to provide exceptional service for your guests. At the same time, because of the outstanding service, you will find that you are no longer keeping up with the Joneses of your local hotel industry, because you will be setting the service standard for quality!

Employees That Look the Part

No matter the hotel, uniforms are a key part of the guest experience. These give your guests a quick way to identify the hotel staff, but uniforms also give your staff a more polished look. But if you depend on your employees to care for their uniforms, you might not always have the polished look that you want. This part of your guest's visual experience needs to be exceptional. Guests notice the littlest details. If your staff looks unkempt, then your guest will wonder about other details around the hotel. You want to make sure they see right from the start that you care about the little details and making sure that your guests are satisfied every time.

In this regard, uniforms for your employees are also another area where you can take advantage of a quality dry-cleaning service. Guests like seeing a sharp, well-dressed staff. It presents your hotel in a better light, particularly with business guests. However, at the same time, uniforms that are not well cared for can have the opposite effect. So you want to be sure the uniforms are being properly cleaned and mended. But if you don't have a vendor that provides outstanding service, then you might find that uniforms aren't the only things being damaged by the vendor.

Do you offer dry-cleaning services to your employees for their uniforms? If so, how is that service performed? Your employees should receive their uniforms back, clean and in good condition, as well as timely, so they can be ready to go on their shift. It reflects poorly on your hotel, in the guest's mind, when staff don't appear at their best. At the same time, you want to make sure that each employee gets back their uniform. Have you ever had a mix-up that meant one of your taller employees was wearing too short pants or a shirt with cuffs that were higher than the wrist? Trying to scramble to make sure they have a well-fitting uniform in time for their shift can be a stressful situation to say the least. Not to mention, it is a reduction of the productivity of your staff, especially if it happens on a regular basis.

Then there is the reality of a poorly cleaned uniform. You can't let an employee go out in that; so again, it is a scramble to outfit them with a uniform that is clean and reflects well on your hotel. But, as many hotel managers can attest, there is so much more that can go wrong with a dry-cleaning service, which can apply to both the guest orders and the uniforms of the hotel staff.

The Challenges of a Dry-Cleaning Service

No matter what service you offer your guests, the point is to provide outstanding service. You want to make their stay exceptional because of how smooth it was and how easy it was for them to use the various services and amenities offered by the hotel. But as you know, once a hotel has to include an outside vendor to the mix, there are plenty of opportunities for your guest to have issues and problems that make them regret staying at your hotel. In that case, their stay was anything but smooth, and can hardly be classified as outstanding!

Adding dry-cleaning to the mix of vendors can be another source of potential challenges. Here are just a few of the potential issues that come up with a dry-cleaning service:

- Clothes get mixed up.
- Items aren't delivered to guests in a timely way.
- There is no accountability for damage to clothing.
- There is no system for delivery of garments to guests.
- Staff uniforms come back mismatched or not properly cleaned.
- Your employees are the point person for guests but lack power to solve issues.

Without a quality system in place, inconsistency for your guests and your employees will exist. Inconsistencies can end up costing you time and money, in terms of dissatisfied guests and frustrated employees. Therefore, it is about more than just picking a vendor; it is about finding the vendor with a system that can be easily added to your own hotel systems, providing outstanding service that your guests will appreciate!

By implementing a system, not just selecting a vendor, you benefit in the following ways:

- Add value for guests, especially business travelers
- Stand out from the local competition
- Increase revenue
- Provide a system that is effective for both guests and employees

Perhaps you hadn't originally planned to add dry-cleaning to your offerings. It's too much trouble, you might think to yourself. The potential for error is high, and our control over the vendor's performance is limited. These objections are based on your previous experiences with other vendors, and the lack of systems that allow for your employees to provide quality service. Throughout the next few chapters, I am going to show you how it is possible to build a relationship with a vendor by implementing a system that brings the best service to your guests.

However, let's talk about the elephant in the room, which is the BNB services offered through the internet. Many hotels find themselves competing on an unlevel playing field, as they have to meet a variety of safety codes, homeland security guidelines, and building/fire regulations, just to name a few. Many individuals who use the BNB services to offer their homes or vacation homes for rent, do not have to meet those same codes and regulations. The result is that the costs for the hotel are going up to meet their compliance requirements, while homeowners continue to enjoy minimal overhead or none at all.

Anticipating what your guests want beforehand, and having those elements in place, can help hotels stand out from the typical BNB offering. Flexibility is also required, as travelers are dealing with a variety of variables, which can include late flights, weather, or even just the difficulty of finding a cab to their lodgings. While the BNB service might offer less expensive accommodations, they often don't offer the amenities of a standard hotel. In fact, they often offer much less. Still, if the services you offer don't provide an excellent experience every time, then a guest will not see them as benefits to staying at a hotel. Thus, the hotels are just competing against each other, but they are also having to compete against these BNB options.

I have talked a lot about the benefits of value-added amenities for your guests. This is one area where you can really make your hotel stand out from the pack, but only if you can find the right vendors to partner with. Below are just a few things you need to ask your vendors before you start working with them:

- How does your system work?
- How will using your system provide value to both my hotel and my guests?
- How does it integrate with my current hotel systems?
- What type of training do you offer my staff on your systems?
- What are the options available to deal with problems or issues?
- Who do I contact to deal with questions, and what is their availability?
- What type of references can you offer from others who have worked with you?

As you can see, it is important to find out not only what they do right, but how they handle the various hiccups that can happen. I make sure that each of my hotels has a list of contacts that allow them to access one of my employees regardless of the time of day. I don't believe in the idea that a problem or issue has to wait until the next day because it is after 5 p.m. Hotels are a 24/7 business, and your vendors need to have a way to provide access in case of problems, regardless of the time of day.

Another key point is how well they have operated with other hotels. In my interviews with various hotel managers, I have found that one of the key issues with vendors is the vendors that cancel at the last minute, or simply don't show up when they are scheduled. For hotels, this can be a huge issue, because they often don't have another vendor that can be a substitution; or if they do find a substitute, the costs go up substantially.

As you can see, I have identified several potential issues with using an outside vendor for any service, but particularly dry-cleaning. Still, it is possible to find the right vendor for your hotel. For vendors, it is key to become part of the solution for the hotel, not part of the problem. However, as a vendor, you are also in a key position to be a problem solver for your hotel clients, as I will demonstrate in the following chapter.

Chapter 3

Position Yourself as a Problem Solver

Managing and caring for a large hotel is a balancing act that involves constantly problem solving. No matter what is going on for a guest, even if it isn't necessarily a service the hotel provides, you find your staff working to help. It is part of the quality customer service that leaves the guest pleased with their experience, but also willing to come back.

Without the right systems in place, however, your staff cannot effectively handle those guest problems, and the guest leaves feeling that the customer service is lacking. When they do that, the impact on your hotel is negative, and it can spread from that guest to other potential ones. We have all met someone who has had a bad hotel experience. For some, the staff was able to address the issues and turn the experience from a negative to a positive. But if your staff is not trained to problem solve, then they won't be able to turn that negative into a positive.

Building a Successful System

One of the primary ways to build a system that is effective is to not stop improving. I refer to it as the Constant Never Ending Improvement (CANI) approach. This approach believes that no system or process is perfect, but can always be improved. Therefore, when you put a system in place, there needs to be a process that allows you to review the procedures of that system on a regular basis, looking for areas where it can be improved. This can mean reducing any redundant steps, or even putting steps in to address issues that may have come up.

Feedback doesn't need to be limited to just a few members of your team. Be willing to hear the voices of every team member, both on what they found that worked, and areas where they thought it could have gone better. If they have suggestions on how to make any process better, then it should be taken seriously. The whole point of evaluating your processes on a regular basis is to always look for ways to improve your guest's experience with your hotel and staff.

When it is clear that you are looking for the best method versus holding onto to a specific way of doing things, just because it has always been done that way, then you will be positioning yourself as a leader for your team. Developing a team requires more than just giving direction. It involves listening to your team and motivating them to get access to their best ideas and skill sets. You want them to feel invested in the outcomes of the team's efforts.

Developing your team reflects on your managerial skills as well, demonstrating that you are able to work with your team to effectively reach goals. Here are just a few principles to keep in mind when working with your staff to get the best from them.

Create a rapport with your staff. If they believe you are approachable, you are more likely to connect with them, and they are more likely to give you their best effort. The converse of this is that your suggestions are likely to be accepted much more readily and then acted on. I always tell my people that they are the most important part of my business, so if they have personal issues at work, then I want to resolve them right away. This is because I recognize that those personal issues can have an impact on their performance and the overall performance of my team. As a service vendor, my team is my business, and I want to keep it tuned to the maximum level. That means helping my staff to resolve a variety of problems. I want to be there for them so that they can be there for me, and so that we can both benefit financially.

The intention is not necessarily reflected in the behavior. Often, the behavior may reflect poorly on an individual, but it is not the individual themselves. Therefore, encourage changes in behavior, regardless of intent. Focus on their behavior, and separate that from the individual themselves.

Everyone has a set of resources and do the best they can with it. Don't be quick to judge your employees, but instead, look for how you can tap into their resources effectively. This could mean acknowledging a weakness and providing the necessary training to assist them in overcoming that weakness, or capitalizing on their strengths and using them in positions that allow them to maximize their skills.

As you can see, there are a variety of ways to work with your staff to build a team, but also acknowledge them as individuals. When you manage from a place of team building, you will see that your employees will respond positively. You will find that their skill sets will grow and help you to meet the needs of your clients in the hotel business. But what value do you bring as a vendor?

The Value Vendors Can Bring

What do you value from your vendors? For most of us, it is communication, professionalism, and a good service or product, with value and fair pricing. However, there are other areas where hotel managers find themselves between a rock and a hard place, in part because of the actions of their vendors in a variety of areas. Here are just a few of those areas.

Timeliness is also a key issue in the hotel business. When a carpet vendor, for instance, promises to show up at a specific time of day, but are hours late or even postpone to another day, it can throw off the entire schedule of the hotel. This is especially true when the hotel is hosting an event and they have only one day to get the carpets cleaned for the event. It must happen on the day scheduled. Hotel managers can often find themselves up against a wall because the vendor is late or postpones, and they must scramble, perhaps paying a higher rate for a rush job, just to meet the timeline for their event.

Quality is another key issue for hotel managers. A vendor may think they are offering a quality product or service, but do their customers agree? Are they meeting the expectations that they set out for their customers? The reality is that many vendors sell a great promise but often under-deliver. However, with the right systems in place, a vendor can sell the right product or service to match their customer's needs, and deliver what they promise.

How to Provide Outstanding Service to Hotels

Another key that I have found in my business is to **see a need and to fill that need**. Many of my hotels have had issues over the years, and I have put myself in the place of being a problem solver for them. I have become the go-to guy for a variety of issues. For example, I had a driver come up to make a delivery at a hotel that had an iron on fire. He immediately notified me, and I contacted the GM. One of the areas that had been damaged was their laundry facilities. As part of my services, I offered to take on the cleaning of their linens and other laundry that they typically handled in house. It was an additional load on my staff for a period of time, but I know that it made an impression on that hotel's GM, in a positive way. We were able to continue offering additional services to that hotel, and have built a long-term relationship from my willingness to make myself available to them.

I have always trained my drivers and other staff to be aware of what is going on at the hotels that we service. This gives us opportunities to provide services that might be outside of the dry-cleaning realm. One of my employees, for example, ran a carpet cleaning business, but he was struggling to get enough clients to keep it running. So he asked me to take it on. I added it to my portfolio and started looking for an opportunity. One came in the form of a vendor that didn't show up, and a hotel that was on a time crunch. They had to have the carpets cleaned before an event, and their back was against the wall. The GM called me, asking if I knew anyone. Since I had the carpet cleaning service as part of my business, I offered my services to help them out of their jam. The result is that I picked up another piece of business from that hotel, and added value for them.

My experience with most hotels is that they want vendors who follow through and offer excellent service every single time. Hotels often do not have the leeway to find another vendor when one ends up failing to deliver, and that puts them into a tight spot with their guests. I have found that by being the go-to guy for my hotel clients, I have been able to increase my business and grow my reputation as a vendor within the industry.

Even if you don't think you can solve the problem, you will be amazed at who you do know and how your network can be put to use for your clients. Even hiring staff can be an opportunity for you to give hotels the advantage of your experience as a vendor working with multiple hotels. While it is a small industry, vendors often bring a different viewpoint, which GMs can find valuable.

The reality is that a vendor is an expert in their own business. But the world doesn't recognize you as an expert unless they talk with you, or if they see you in another position of authority. By this, I mean the world is more likely to see an author as an expert than the man they meet on the street. If you offer a unique service as a vendor, then consider writing about that service and what it can offer your potential clients. Set yourself up as the expert in your industry. Be willing to speak at seminars and conventions with other industry members. Doing so will help you to make a quality impression on your potential clients, who will see you as someone who can provide knowledgeable and quality service for their business.

I have found, over the years, that there are certain personality types that need to be considered as you are building your team. One of the best ways that I have been able to understand my hires and team better is through a personality test. There are multiple types of tests, but according to experts, there are four basic personality types. As individuals, we tend to lean toward one or two traits and are weaker in the other two traits.

When you can identify an individual's stronger traits, then it gives you a greater insight into what motivates them, what they care about, and even how they might react to different forms of communication. Think about your team for a moment. Do you have several millennials? How about among your managers? Are there several baby boomers? How do they react to a communication system that limits face-to-face time with employees, but involves more texts or quick chats via a cell phone? These generational differences can also factor into how individuals of your team function with each other.

Using the BANK system, which is an acronym for the four personality types of Blueprint, Action, Nurturing, and Knowledge, an employer can learn about a potential or current employee's strengths, and learn how to maximize them. At the same time, it helps you as a manager to become a better communicator with your team, because you can find the style that works best for your team. Throughout the next few chapters, I will be talking about how my system can be implemented into your hotel. Still, without an understanding of what motivates your team, and how to reach them to connect with that motivation, it can be hard to get the best from them.

Chapter 4

How My System to Service Hotels Was Created

As part of my professional career and entrepreneurship, I attend to a variety of trainings almost every month of the year. Clearly, I prefer to stay busy with my business, but I never want my business to grow stagnant. I like to have ideas from different kinds of industry professionals on how to improve my business. This constant learning and improvement have always been a cornerstone to my professional career. Never assume that you have the best idea, but be open to hearing what others have to say, and taking advantage of the wisdom they have gained through their own experiences.

When I was at the training at Pick Potentials, it was suggested to create a seminar and teach people how to do a task or provide a service. Starting from this idea, I began to build my system. Once the recession hit in 2007/2008, the need to find another way to earn my living came into play. Programmers weren't necessarily in need, but hotels needed ways to drive business into their industry by providing added value for their guests. At the same time, it is an industry that thrives best with systems, so my training and experience were a natural fit to this vibrant section of the travel world.

I had been drawn to the clothing business, ever since I made that first outfit for myself back in college. I had even moved into the garment industry as a programmer, creating systems to fulfill orders and also get supplies, such as cloth, where they needed to go. Throughout my time in the industry, I was introduced to the dry-cleaning business.

Dry-Cleaning Becomes My Industry

When you look at the history of dry-cleaning, it started around the idea of individuals not having their own laundries. So you packed up your clothes and you took them to the local laundry, where they were cleaned and pressed before you picked them up. Typically, it was a once-a-week process, but there were those businesses or individuals that had an outfit or clothing into the laundry on a daily basis, such as hotels.

Now I have to take you back in the laundry business for a minute. Back then, we didn't have hot water tanks and washers or dryers that did the work for us. That was a period that involved boiling water, using a paddle to agitate the clothes, hand scrubbing to get the hard stains out, hand rinsing before hanging them out to dry, and then hand pressing.

Today, much of this process has been automated. Now we have machines that do a majority of the washing work, although we still have to treat for stains and handle any repairs as needed. But as dry-cleaning has progressed, there was the introduction of chemicals into the process. Over time, exposure to those chemicals can have a negative effect on your clients and your employees. I looked at the process and was trying to figure out a way to reduce the chemical impact but still provide the same quality cleaning process.

That's when I began building my GoGreen system. The process allows us to reduce the chemical load on the clothes, and give our clients an even better experience in terms of how their clothes look, feel, and smell. Our system is geared toward creating a great experience for our clients every single time, and that includes how their clothes look and feel when they get them back. How many of us have gotten clothes back from the dry cleaners and immediately could smell the chemicals? I knew that providing the best possible service for guests and others was by making sure their clothes smelled great.

Another area that my hotel guests pointed out was repairs and damage done to clothes. As a former self-trained tailor, I know that providing quality repairs can extend the life of the clothes. For travelers on the go, it can be hard to get those repairs done, especially if you only have a few outfits with you. But if you are using the dry-cleaning service, you want to make sure that your clothes aren't damaged during that service. My system addresses both of these areas through our tracking and intake system.

Using my system, we are able to determine if any buttons are loose, and correct that before we return your garments. Additionally, we document any damage to the clothes prior to the cleaning process, and address any issues that we can. At the end of the process, the clothes are checked again, to be sure that no new damage has occurred that will need to be addressed. Thus, when the clothes are returned to your guests, they are in great shape and ready to wear.

The point is to make it an experience that adds value to your guests' stay. Throughout the years in this business, I have found ways to create a system that can easily be integrated into any hotel and provide them consistent and quality service. I don't believe that any vendor starts their business with the idea that they are going to provide poor quality service. Yet it often happens, because they don't create systems that support the quality of service they are trying to provide. Over time, their employees rush to meet deadlines, and they might skip key steps that can have a negative impact on the service they provide. The reality is that they aren't anticipating challenges, as I will discuss next.

Building a System With Quality in Mind

Creating a quality system means finding a way to anticipate the problems that can occur during the process. When it comes to dry-cleaning, one of the biggest potential challenges is the number of individuals that play a part in getting the clothes cleaned, pressed, and back to the guests in a timely fashion.

The reality is that the more individuals that are part of a system, the greater the room for error. Therefore, it is key to identify a process and then train the members of the team to do it the same way every time. By doing so, it is easier to identify and find an error if something is not done properly, because you can follow the process and find the breakdown.

Another key to the success of any system is accountability. Are your hotel staff held accountable for following a system? Do they have to sign off on each step? Can you follow them through the process, or do you find there are gaps where you might not be able to confirm a step was completed? Additionally, are there steps that have over time become so automatic to certain employees that they aren't documented?

If you can't follow the process from one step to another, you have the potential for errors to creep in, and for your guests to be unhappy with the service they receive at your hotel. When you add a vendor into the mix, it can create even more unknowns. There are multiple questions that come up. Here are just a few:

- How will their system integrate with yours?
- What are the levels of accountability and tracking?
- What are the consequences if they don't deliver as promised?
- Am I going to have a contact that I can access easily, or will it just be frustrating, with time lost in finding a solution to my guest's problem?
- Do we have to learn as we go, or will your training be comprehensive, answering all my questions?
- Will I feel comfortable with the system by the time your training is complete for myself and my employees?

Vendors can be an unknown in the world of hotels, which can greatly affect how well they are able to provide service to their guests. One of the realities of the hotel business is timing. They are under time constraints that can't be pushed back: a guest may only stay one night; a wedding is happening, over a two-day period at most; and conventions may only be a few days in length. There is no second chance to make a first impression with these guests. Everything has to run smoothly, and the vendors need to play their part in the process.

As a hotel GM, how many times have you had a schedule of vendors for a specific event, only to have one vendor back out at the last minute? Not only does it throw your schedule off, but it also makes it virtually impossible to find a replacement vendor who can perform in the tight deadline. Suddenly, you are up against an unhappy guest and an increasing vendor cost, as the rates have gone up significantly for the last-minute replacement, if one can be found. Vendors clearly need to be road-tested for quality, but at the same time, they will give you clues about how well they will perform during your initial meetings.

Here are a few areas that might show if your vendor can actually deliver or not:

- Can they train your employees on how to perform their process, or do they provide a manual with all the steps?
- Is there a system, or do you just have to trust their people and hope for the best?
- When you book with your vendor, do you have people assigned to your hotel, or is it someone new every time?
- During an event, do you have a point person with the vendor who is on call, or do you find the phones are heading straight to voicemail?

When it comes to choosing a vendor, you need to feel comfortable that they will perform and add value to your brand. If they don't, it isn't their reputation that will suffer, but your own. Guests don't recognize that vendors provide services within the hotel. They see all services as being provided by the hotel, and rate their experience with the hotel on those services. Thus, your vendor choices are key to making a good impression on your guests and bringing them back again and again.

Additionally, your vendor should be providing the necessary parts of their system to your hotel. If you are buying a lot of additional equipment just to integrate their system, then it might be a sign that the vendor isn't really prepared to provide a quality service to your hotel. During the installation and integration process, how does the vendor handle hiccups? Are they prepared, or is it clear that they are winging it?

From experience with a variety of vendors, those that provide quality service are prepared for a variety of challenges. They are ready and able to address any concerns. Additionally, they do their homework and research about your hotel and its setup prior to installation. Thus, when it is time to do the installation of the system, they aren't winging it, but have created a training that works for your hotel, and have adjusted their system to meet your needs. If there are issues during the installation phase, they are available to address them. You aren't left to your own devices.

Clearly, providing a quality service is about more than the system itself. It is about how well that system integrates, the training process, and how well the installation goes. A vendor also needs to be available to their clients, even after the initial installation. A client should never feel as if they have been abandoned by their vendor.

Therefore, as a hotel, it is key to find the right vendors to provide those value-added services to your guests, while at the same time, adding value to your reputation. Over the next few chapters, I will be discussing my training and how it is implemented for my team, as well as the hotel staff and how it can impact your hotel by bringing value to your guests in one of the key potential service areas, laundry and dry-cleaning, especially for those who travel frequently on business.

Chapter 5

How to Train Your Employees

Training is key to the success of any good team. The reality is that your team will grow and perform at its best when it has the opportunity to gain new skills and flex the ones they currently have. But if a training isn't well planned and doesn't give the students an opportunity to practice what they are learning, then the results will often be a waste of time and resources, but not well-trained employees that are ready to execute a service or produce a quality product.

Yet I have seen time and time again that most training programs are limited to indoctrinating new employees on systems and processes, with little training or refreshers offered to the rest of the staff. Overwhelming your new employees and overloading them with a large amount of information is not likely to result in a quality employee, especially if they are not in a position that allows for retraining or chances to refresh their skills and knowledge about the systems or processes. If changes occur, how are they communicated to the staff?

Many times, it becomes a trial and error for the staff themselves, and a struggle to keep quality employees, because they become overwhelmed by the information, changes, and lack of concrete training. Therefore, while training is key, it needs to be more than just one or two seminars. It needs a plan for execution in a way that benefits the employees and makes it an effective training. Also, you need to remember that training is ongoing, so you need to make sure that you are addressing that within your training plan, both short and long term.

So before you start a training process, it is critical to have the goal of the training in mind, and a quality training method in place. Below are just a few key points to keep in mind when training your staff or preparing a training program.

Shaping and Defining Your Team

In order to train your staff to get the best results possible, it is important to have an overall training plan for your team. You need to first define the various departments and what you want them to accomplish. This will include identifying the skill sets that the managers of each department will need. That list can then help you to shape and define the roles of each department manager or leader.

This could also mean reshaping the organizational structure of your team. Perhaps you can see an area that is struggling, and find that by transferring responsibilities, you can achieve better results. It could also mean that you are empowering those who weren't previously managers to take on that role. At the same time, it could also mean that current managers no longer have the skills needed to effectively reach the goals of their department. Therefore, you need to be logical and take the emotion out of your decisions. It is what is best for the company and the department, not necessarily what is best for just one individual. When you focus on what is best for the team, the individuals of the team benefit as a result.

Once you have those roles defined, you need to identify the individuals in your company who match those roles. Those individuals need to be trained in the key areas that they might be lacking, for them to successfully manage their assigned departments. When you move them into their new roles, recognize that they might bring a different perspective, which could further define the goals and processes of the department and team. It could mean that you make adjustments right from the start, but the results could mean benefits to your bottom line.

During this training period, you can create the manuals necessary for each department to function properly. This includes documenting the processes and procedures, even the ones that might seem fairly straight forward and common sense. Let me give you an example. If you are running a banquet, but your banquet manager is ill and she is the only one that knows how to order the chairs, then you may find yourself with an event and no chairs. Although it might be a common-sense step, the reality is that there is a process for every step of any service or product. Your job is to make sure that all those steps are clearly documented for another individual to follow.

During the training process, it is important to make sure that multiple individuals are trained in the various procedures. This will create a redundancy factor that can assist you in running the department should any of the managers or key personnel be sick or otherwise unavailable. The point of redundancy is that each department can deliver the best service to your customers every time, regardless of who is available in the department at any given point.

Training manuals are a key part of building this redundancy. They provide a road map for various team members to follow, thus allowing your departments to provide consistent service and products. After all, if each department were to deliver based on what they decided was the policy or procedure of the moment, then there would not be the consistency and quality that draws and keeps customers.

There is another use for training. It can be the basis of empowering the success of your team. Look at how the various members of your team function with each other. What are their strengths, and what skills do they each bring to the table? Training methods can be used to bring those strengths out even further, by complimenting them, or even by assisting team members to build a strength from a defined weakness or missing skill set.

When the employees of your team feel as if you are investing in their individual success, then they will feel empowered to devote more of their energy and skill sets to build up the team. Investing in the members of your team builds a strong base for your company. While there are definitely overhead costs involved in training members of your team, it is equally clear that the proper training can mean your team is in the position to continually improve your processes, bringing the best service possible to your guests and customers.

Never Assume You Can't Improve

Providing better service is part of a CANI type of mentality for your team. Empowering them with the proper training will allow them find those areas that can be improved. As I have discussed, there is no system that cannot be improved upon. But if your team doesn't feel invested in their work, then they are not likely to look hard for those areas of improvement or the solutions to solve various issues that come up during the course of daily business.

Are there specific areas that you have found your team consistently struggling to excel? They can be some of the first places that you build your training sessions around. These sessions can include webinars, classes, or even team exercises. The point is to build a sense of connection, while acknowledging the strengths of the other members of your team. Millennials are one example of how teams have become more important than even the typical traditional hierarchy of corporations. When your training works to build that sense of teamwork, you can benefit from the power that comes from combining various skill sets.

You can also use these training sessions to get ideas from your team about what is working and what is not. It can be surprising to find that many individuals in your team have ideas that can improve the process, but you don't have a way for those ideas to be expressed and collected. Do not assume that just because one employee doesn't have a management position in your company, that their input is not valuable. It is possible that the solution that you are looking for is right there, just waiting for you to collect it from your team members.

It goes along with the idea of being a good listener. When your team feels that you care about them as individuals and as part of your team, then they will feel more comfortable coming to you, with not only their ideas but also concerns about areas in your system that might not be working as well or downright failing. Keep in mind that you can't be everywhere in your company, but your team is a natural set of eyes and ears that can help you to identify processes that are successful, and ways to transfer that success to the departments that might be struggling.

Also, when you implement a new system, be sure that you get your team's input. They can tell you if key areas of the system are working or if there are details missing in the training that might need to be addressed in the future. Want to find out how complete your manuals are? Have someone from a different department come and try to complete a process from that manual. If they are successful, then it is clear that you have a well-defined process. If they can't manage it, then you might need to provide additional detail or even consider overhauling how the process is completed. The test can also suggest areas where the process might be improved, even if it is well-defined, just because the employee provides a new set of eyes and perspective on the process.

Another area that can help to build up your team is creating goals and then offering incentives that benefit the whole team. Your employees will be able to see that working together can help them all to achieve greater goals than they could as individuals. Building a team mentality often requires that the exercises and milestones of the team are built around the strengths of the whole team. If an individual doesn't feel their skills are needed, they are not likely to be invested, and that often means that you, as the boss, are not receiving the best that you can from them.

As you can see, training is about more than just imparting a new set of skills or teaching a new process or system. It can also be a critical way to build up your team and create the unity that allows you to provide the best service to your clients and guests, each and every time.

Redundancy is Key

Have you ever had a key employee not come into work? While the reason could be the flu or a family emergency, the result can often be a mad scramble to fill in their position and make sure that the whole team and your clients are not let down because that slot is empty for a day or even longer. How can you avoid having that mad scramble? The key is redundancy. But how can that redundancy be achieved? The best method is through your team training system.

How to Provide Outstanding Service to Hotels

Every one of your employees should be trained to handle not only their main task but several other tasks in different areas, which will create redundancy. The reason is that if somebody is sick or decides to leave your company, you can move someone else into their position, thus allowing your process to run without interruptions. Each of my employees are trained in 5 to 6 additional tasks outside of their main specialty. This means that while you might have a specialty, you can easily be pulled to cover another area when necessary. However, to make sure that this system will work when you need it, you need to schedule regular refresher courses for your staff, allowing them to keep their skills current on the various positions they may be called on to complete.

When you work with hotels, you must pick up and deliver guest clothes on a same day timeframe. It means you have 3–4 hours between the time the clothes are brought to the store and the time they are heading back to hotels. Most of the tasks can be done in parallel to increase speed, while maintaining the same quality that your clients and guests expect. I often switch my employees from their area of main responsibility, to different areas for a few days or weeks, and then bring them back to perform their main tasks. This allows me to address times when our workload increases, as we can adjust to meet those needs by assigning multiple individuals to similar tasks.

Imagine for a moment that you can put 4–5 employees on a bottle neck task to run it on a parallel basis for a short period, but then bring them back to their original tasks when the bottle neck is overcome. This kind of flexibility is also key when taking on new clients or potentially large orders on any given day of the week. For example, you may find that Mondays are a particularly busy day, as employee uniforms from the weekend come in, along with various items from guests. Therefore, it might end up being the most important day to make sure you have scheduled extra staff into their redundancy positions, to make sure that all tasks will be completed in a timely fashion. Outstanding service, every time, is a matter of scheduling and training, as well as having a great system in place.

At the same time, it is key to make sure that your staff members feel appreciated as part of your team. Training will only take you so far. Therefore, it is also key to make sure that you schedule time for the critical aspects of team building. This includes celebrating the success of your team in meeting sales goals or deadlines.

Celebrating the Successes

I always celebrate success, and work on our team building, because it helps my staff to feel invested in the progress of the business. When we have a new client, I bring in lunch and discuss with my team how we achieved it because of their hard work and quality efforts. It helps my employees to see the direct results of their efforts, and it inspires them to keep it up. I can tell my client all day long how good my team is, but if we do not perform, then I will lose that new client and all the business from them. I always tell my team the real stories from hotel managers, and the hotel's reasons why they choose to change their provider and go with us.

Keep in mind, for my first few hotels, I just had a system and hoped they would be willing to give it a try. When you are just setting out, it can be difficult to get that first client. But once you do, keeping them involves making sure that they receive the best possible service. When a client has received excellent service, they will recommend you to others. Word of mouth in our industry is a powerful thing, and it works both ways. When a client has just one or two negative experiences, then typically that means the vendor's contract will be canceled. After losing just a few clients, it can be hard to win others, and even harder to hold onto the ones that you have. My point is that there is more to getting and keeping a client than a sales pitch. The quality of the service or product you provide will impact your ability to hold onto your clients long into the future.

As hoteliers, you can relate. Guests today have plenty of ways to express their opinions about their experience at your hotel, good or bad. The internet and social media have given them the ability to express their displeasure almost instantaneously. I believe it is key to make sure that you treat every interaction with your clients as if it is their first impression of you and your team.

At the same time, it is key to stress with your team how much your reputation rides on them and how they do their jobs on a daily basis. One of my favorite examples is of a GM who was using our service and was down to his last shirt, and noticed that one of the buttons was broken. He didn't have time to get a new shirt or even to get this one fixed. How would he look, and what would this do to his confidence in that meeting, but most importantly, how would he feel about our team in the future? If we do well with a GM's clothes, then we will pick up his guests' clothes and will be working with his hotel. But if he has a bad experience, then we won't be working with his hotel in the future. Managers are willing to be guinea pigs, but knowing that, it is key to make sure the service is exceptional.

When I talk with the managers and GMs for the first time, I promise that this will not happen to them with our service. My team has not made me a liar, but has always delivered exceptional service. For a hotel, quality service from a vendor can help them secure a repeat guest, particularly from those who travel frequently on business. But when a vendor fails a hotel, it can end up costing that hotel hundreds, if not thousands of dollars, in terms of potential lost revenue. Not to mention, it can also translate to a hit on their online reputation. The vendor will also lose, because not only will they not likely have that hotel as a client, but they may also not get additional hotels because the vendor's reputation has also taken a hit. Remember, the hotel industry is a relatively small one, so ruining your reputation with one GM can mean ruining it with others. Word of mouth is a key part of this industry.

Another way to get your team invested in delivering a quality service or product is to have them take into account the financial impact that losing a client will mean for them. I am honest with my employees that a lost client can impact the size of our staff. Jobs are created or lost based on the number of hotels we are servicing. So the better they perform, the greater the job security for everyone on the team. Quality is a team expectation, because we all have something invested in the outcome of keeping our clients satisfied.

What is your team's philosophy? It is important to have one, because it provides another method to create a bond within your team. With my team, our motto is "We Are Better Because We Try Harder." It is a philosophy that I repeat with my team on a regular basis, and I support my philosophy with real-life examples so that they can make it their philosophy too. When you empower your team, they will be a part of your success, because they will see it as part of their own success.

Have your clients given you compliments regarding the level of customer service they have received? What do you do with those compliments? It is key to share those with your team. The reason is that individuals work better when they are motivated. What is better motivation than hearing, "Good job," with details about what you did well? Your team will benefit from hearing those compliments that you receive from clients, because it is a source of motivation for them.

Some of the compliments I have received include, "Your manager is a pro," "Your presser is excellent," and "You have the best quality shirts." My team enjoys hearing these compliments. They feel appreciated when they hear what our clients have said, but they also feel encouraged to maintain that standard of excellence and even exceed it!

The other motivation for your team is financial. If they aren't able to work hard and earn more money, then they aren't going to be motivated to keep up a high level of excellence. Therefore, having financial rewards is key to keeping a quality team. They need to know that if you are doing well financially, it will filter down to them as well. However, a team is only as successful as its weakest link. When one employee underperforms, others must step in to take up the slack, and this can mean that you find yourself with a disgruntled team over the long haul. After all, you can't overwork your best employees and expect them to maintain a high quality of service.

Everyone gets worn out. The point of the team is to make sure that no one individual or group carries most of the weight of providing quality service. In the end, the team suffers if the individual members can't work together. That means everyone bringing their best to the job every day. I want to point out that as human beings, it isn't always possible. Our personal lives come with us to the job. I have found that having an open-door policy with my staff has allowed me to know what is going on in their lives. If they are having trouble at home with a sick kid or family issues, knowing can help me to moderate their assignment, so that I get the best from them and they don't have the stress of their job on top of everything else.

Know the Members of Your Team

Getting to know your team makes them feel as if they are more than just a number to your company; they feel that they really matter. Time has proven again and again how important it is that your team feel their own personal value to the company they work for. Doing this is a key part of building a team that will contribute to the long-term success of your business, because they are invested too.

When it came to creating my system, I found that there were plenty of areas where key steps could be skipped or missed. Controls needed to be put into place to make sure that if one individual missed something, it would be caught be someone else. A form of checks and balances had to be created, but it was key to make sure that those checks didn't end up creating more work than necessary and slow down the process. They had to make sense within the process itself.

In my work as a programmer, triple control was key to the success of anything that I put together. This meant that there were multiple ways to reduce mistakes or problems with any system or program. No matter what system you are putting into place, it is key that you have checks and balances in place to make sure that nothing falls through the cracks.

When it came to handling the dry-cleaning for any hotel, I implemented a triple control system that meant clothes could pass through multiple hands, but that the system would consistently deliver a quality service every time, because every employee followed the checks and balances of the system.

Let's start at the front counter. Every employee at our front line has to check the incoming clothes for stains, discoloration, and any pre-existing damage on the garments, which could include loose buttons and strings or holes. If they find anything, then they will note it on the ticket with the garment. Once it moves on to the spotter, the process is repeated again. Each individual will notice something different, so this decreases the chances that we will miss something before the cleaning process begins.

After cleaning, the check is performed again, and then a 4th time during the pressing process. The assembly employee checks these details, making sure that stains had been taken care of, and any repairs that were required to be done were completed. Then other details that are part of our quality control check are completed as the garments are bagged for delivery. During this process, our employees always put their initials that they completed each of the steps. Doing so allows us to find the individual who made a mistake, if one happens. Therefore, an employee feels accountable to do their job well, because they can be held to a set of standards, and their work can be traced through the system. At the same time, if you don't have consequences in place for the work not being completed correctly, then the team won't see the quality control system as something that will hold them accountable.

Rewards for excellent work, and consequences for underperformance, need to be enforced equally. If you are great at rewarding your team, but bad at holding them accountable when problems arise, then the quality of your service can be negatively impacted. Keeping the balance in place is key to providing the best possible service for your clients every single time, and building a team that provides outstanding service.

Another key to my system is making sure that there are paths to follow clothes throughout the process. One such key is the manifest. It becomes the key to efficient delivery of garments once the delivery is returned to the hotel, as you will see. The manifest for the hotel's delivery is also the key to making sure that every guest gets back their garments in a timely fashion. Plus, if something appears to be missing, the manifest can help us to quickly discover where the missing garments are and what happened to them. This means that the guest often never knows that there was any issue to begin with.

Prior to the delivery, the clothes are loaded on the rack in the order on the manifest. Then they are loaded into the truck into that same order. The manager checks the manifest against what is loaded on the truck, and then signs off on the manifest. There are always two copies of the manifest, one for my team and one for the hotel. This allows us both to know the order the clothes arrived in and determine if the entire order was delivered correctly.

The driver checks the manifest, both when he loads the truck and when he unloads the order at the hotel. When the clothes are delivered, they are placed on a delivery rack in the same order as they are listed on the manifest. Then a hotel employee checks the manifest while the driver reads off the parts of the order. The hotel employee marks the manifest, verifying that they received everything; then they sign both manifest copies.

If the hotel then delivers orders to the guests and find something is missing, the manifest can be used as proof that all the garments made it to the hotel. Often, once the manifest is pulled, the manager is able to talk with the hotel employee who signed off, and locate the missing items. This means that the guest receives great service, and the hotel looks fantastic. As a vendor, your job is to fit seamlessly into the hotel and make sure that you are assisting them in providing the best possible service to their guests. When you don't, the hotel will move on to find the vendor that provides what they need. Training employees and building a strong team is key to being the vendor that stands the test of time.

Hotels have found that by using the manifest to deliver to the rooms in the order they are listed on it, then they can quickly locate a missing order by backtracking to the previous room. Often, the garments were left with the last order by mistake. My system has been put in place in multiple hotels, and the issue of missing garments has been virtually eliminated because of the manifest and quality control checks that I have put in place. My team is accountable for doing their job right every time, but they also see the rewards of a job well done.

The point of any system is to reduce or eliminate errors. When I created my system, I realized that adding these checks and balances could make any system fool-proof. As my business has grown and I have begun to offer additional services to hotels, I have continued working to improve the system. No matter what you are doing, the point is to continually improve and look for the ways to get better, and make your business stand out from the crowd.

Hotels offer a variety of services to their guests. For business travelers, in particular, hotels are a home away from home. That means they need access to technology, food, laundry and dry-cleaning, as well as a clean and comfortable room. Hotels deliver exceptional service when they anticipate a guest's needs and have a solution in place before the guest even checks in.

As a vendor, the same applies to me and my team. We need to anticipate the needs of our hotel clients, and address them in a timely fashion. After all, they don't deal in delays, especially when they have a guest who is checking out shortly, standing in front of them expecting results. While you might not always see the emergency, as a vendor, you have to treat your clients as if their emergency is your emergency. That being said, I have made it a point to try to address the needs of my clients before they even realize the need. At the same time, I also try to make sure that we are always available to address any questions that they may have. As you will see in the following chapters, part of our hotel training is focused on those moments when something has gone wrong, and how our system addresses it.

I can tell many stories about how hotels that offer dry-cleaning services have been turned off because the vendor would make multiple mistakes, leaving the hotel with an unhappy guest. Yet they would stay with the vendor, unlike other areas of their business, because they didn't believe that the service could be improved on. I have changed that with my system, but with the right system and training in place, any problem area in your hotel can be made into a service that your guests appreciate and may even rave about to their fellow travelers.

While the vendor might have a solid team, how can you make sure that your employees within the hotel are following the system for maximum success?

Chapter 6

How to Train Hotel Employees

My years in the hotel business have taught me many lessons. But one thing that has really stood out to me is how key it is to have the right people in the right positions. For example, if you don't have friendly and outgoing individuals in the front desk area, guests could be turned off right away. When you have those friendly and outgoing individuals, they can set your guests at ease and make the process of checking in or out and answering questions that much easier. Comfortable guests are more likely to return, and also give positive reviews online and in person.

The same holds true for a vendor who is providing a service to a hotel. If we don't have the right people in place, then we won't be able to provide the best service possible. Our hotels need to feel comfortable with us to give us those positive reviews to their fellow hoteliers, but also to keep using our services. However, once we drop the clothes off to the hotel, it is up to the hotel employees to finish providing the guest an excellent experience by promptly delivering the items to their rooms.

Implementing the System in Your Hotel

Does your current vendor provide training in their system and processes to your staff? If they don't have a system that includes training for your employees, then it is possible that during the transition from the vendor to the hotel, there could be problems. That is why I include training for the housekeeping and front desk staff as part of my start up with any new hotel.

In doing so, I have found that I have been able to eliminate most of the issues regarding guests' clothes, and give the hotel a service that satisfies their guests repeatedly.

One of the best ways to truly integrate with a hotel is to have a comprehensive training for your hotel employees. This allows them to understand how the system works, but also the role that they play in its success. I am amazed at how often companies do not clue their employees in on the bigger picture, but still expect their employees to remain invested in their jobs and the company.

The first thing I ask a new client is if they have had employee clothes or guest clothes cleaned by a dry-cleaning service, and if it was done to their satisfaction. If it wasn't, I ask them to identify the continuing point of frustration or the repeating error. One of the major issues seems to be misplaced clothes. It is often the case that the clothes have not been delivered or were mis-tagged. My system addresses these issues with the quality control checks. Additionally, the manifest provides a way to track what has been delivered and what was not.

One hotel, for example, was looking for one piece that was for a guest. The hotel called me and claimed that the one piece had not been delivered. I asked if they had delivered all the orders according to the manifest. They said that yes, the orders had been delivered based on the manifest. I told them to go to the room right before the guest room that was missing its order. It turned out that the order had been accidently delivered with the previous order, so it was missing when the hotel staff reached the next room. Over time, the hotel staff have learned to check these things first before making the call, thus leading to higher guest satisfaction and also making the job of the hotel staff that much easier.

Another way the manifest is key is when it comes to tracking what was in a client's order. One example was an order that had pieces for a guest and his girlfriend. However, the housekeeping staff accidently separated the garments before delivery. Thus, when the girlfriend's clothes were not delivered, but the guest received his, it was clear that something had gone wrong. After talking with the delivery staff and the receiving staff member from the hotel, we were able to locate the missing garment in a closet downstairs. The items were delivered, and the hotel staff was able to resolve the issue to the guest's satisfaction.

Still, there has to be a sense that the GM can walk into the process and easily find what they need. As part of my training, I work directly with the GM of the hotel to get them familiar with the process and how their staff will need to follow specific steps to ensure that the system works at its optimal level. The hotel staff, of course, need to have a point person that they typically will deal with, which is often my delivery driver. However, if several people are trained to be that point person, then they will also have that built-in redundancy that I have found to be so key to the success of my business. After all, a driver may show up with a delivery, and the regular front desk person is out sick. No matter who is at the front desk, they should be able to follow the steps to achieve the best service possible for their guests.

As I mentioned previously in the team building chapter, it is also important to consider building in retraining or refresher courses for the staff. These will allow new staff members to be trained on the system, but also make sure that long time employees are kept up to date on any changes to the system or upgrades. Remember, the point is to always be looking for ways to get better!

The hotel team also needs to be invested in making sure all the processes and services offered by the hotel are being performed in a way that translates into outstanding service for the guests. This means taking into account ideas that the hotel staff might offer to improve the efficiency of various processes or even your particular system. Growth comes through listening and really hearing the points that the other party has to offer.

Yet within the process of implementing your system into a new hotel, there is the question of the administrative paperwork that will be created. I am talking about billing and invoicing.

Accommodating the Needs of the Hotel Administration

As part of my system, I also take into account how the hotel functions in terms of accounting and billing. I can then make adjustments to break the statements down by department, or even create a separate manifest for their guests and employees. This can make it easier for the hotel to bill the guests, while also keeping their section of the bill separate for the employee uniforms.

I work with the administrative personnel to find the best method for their hotel. Remember, the size of the hotel and the chain hotel's requirements also may need to be considered when determining the best invoicing option for a new hotel client. Taking the time for your client at this early stage in the process can set the tone for your relationship going forward, helping the client to feel as if they are your number one client.

A benefit of the additional separate invoice is that you can offer large group dry-cleaning options to your guests who might be here as part of a convention taking place in the hotel or the local area. By promoting these types of services, the hotel is able to foresee a need of the guest, and meet it before the guest even inquires. Plus, it adds value for the organizers of the convention, because they can let their attendees know the option is available. They are more likely to book with the hotel for the event if they see that the hotel offers more amenities for their attendees, while providing excellent service to the convention overall.

Another key part of the training process for hotel staff is to check the drop off box frequently. Doing so will make sure that all orders are picked up on time by the driver, and that they will be able to be returned at the right time to meet the needs of the guest. Many guests aren't at a hotel for multiple nights, so the plus of a dry-cleaning service in a hotel is the same day aspect. If the front desk staff do not regularly check the drop off box, they could be putting a guest order at risk of not making the same day return, and thus having to deal with an unhappy guest.

My training program for new hotel clients addresses these issues and many more. The point of any system is to address all the needs of the client and make sure their staff can easily follow the process. The hotel staff shouldn't be in the dark about their part in the system, but also should understand how the process works as a whole. This way, they may be able to address the concerns of the guest before even contacting the vendor. However, I let my clients know that we are always available to address their concerns or questions, even if they aren't directly related to the dry-cleaning business.

As a result, I have been able to grow my business in surprising ways, but also address the concerns of my clients. When you as a vendor are able to work with your hotels in this way, you become a team with your clients. This means that you are both invested in the outcome of the service, each and every time that it is provided to a guest.

Throughout this process, you have been able to see how a combination of training, listening to your clients' needs, and being available to your clients is key to the success of any hotel/vendor relationship. However, I believe that in order for the vendor and hotel to work in perfect sync, they need to see themselves as a team and act accordingly. In the next chapter, I will address how to create a one-team service for dry-cleaning, but the steps could be used to create a team with any vendor that your hotel uses.

Chapter 7

How to Create One-Team Hotel Dry-Cleaning

The beauty of any system is when it can create one team between the client and the vendor. When that happens, the vendor is able to assist their client to provide excellent service at every opportunity. My system is meant to create that one team for hotel dry-cleaning service, but it can be applied to any system where a vendor is used to perform a service for the hotel.

How do we create this team atmosphere for our hotel clients? The first and most important way is to be available. When I first begin my relationship with one of my hotels, I go through the whole process with the employees that will be working with the dry-cleaning service at the hotel itself. I also work with the managerial staff so that they are familiar with the system, even if they don't actually participate in the process on a daily basis.

This means explaining the whole process that a piece of clothing goes through before it is returned to the guest of the hotel. At the same time, the training for the housekeepers and front desk staff helps to resolve most of the issues that might occur with guest clothes. Essentially, the training will help them feel confident in the process and make it easier for them to successfully deal with any guest concerns and keep them satisfied.

The training that I give to the hotel staff also will end up saving the hotel staff time. The reason is that they won't be calling the vendor to attempt to solve any issues, because they will have the knowledge to address them right away. Every call you have to make will just add on to the time it takes to solve the issue for your guest, and that is also more time for them to get irritated with your hotel and its staff.

The faster an issue is resolved for a guest, the better the guest experience, and the more likely they will give the hotel a favorable review. Throughout my training, I give the hotel staff the tools to handle a variety of issues in the fastest and most beneficial way for both the guests and the employees. After all, no one likes to be the one who has to give a guest bad news or say the words, "We can't."

So how can we provide a way to give your hotel staff the benefit of our knowledge as a vendor at any time? It starts with our manual binder.

The Critical Path: The Manual Binder

What are some of the methods that we have put into place to assist the hotel staff? The first is the binder. This is my manual for the hotel, and it is the critical reference point for all procedures and processes, from the time the clothes are picked up to the time they are delivered back to the guest. One of the key parts of my process is to be available to my hotel managers. Vendors who don't make themselves available to their clients can find that they are dealing with more fires than they really need to, come Monday morning.

Within my binder for my hotels, they have an order of individuals to call if they have a problem that they can't resolve. The first person on that list is typically the driver who just dropped off the order. Next, I put myself on the list. After me, there are several different managers. In all, there are at least five individuals who are available to the hotel staff at any given point in time. There are a few reasons for this. One, by having multiple contact points, the hotel is sure to get in contact with someone in a timely fashion. Remember, in the hotel business, time costs money and guest goodwill.

Two, the reality is that not every individual will be in a position to answer every call that comes through. By providing multiple contact points, the hotel is always going to find someone available to help them find the solution they need in order to satisfy the guest. Additionally, all of these individuals are empowered to find a solution for the hotel, allowing for seamless service and instant problem solving.

The next key point within the binder is the daily log of what has been picked up and what has been dropped off. Here is where the hotel is able to keep a log of the manifests, as well as the guest orders. However, guest orders need to be handled promptly. By training the housekeeping staff, I eliminate the problem that occurred at one hotel in my portfolio.

The hotel cleaning staff received the bag of clothes from a guest, but they did not get the bag to the front desk until the next day. Now the guests were looking for their clothes, but they hadn't even left the hotel yet for the cleaning process. I have to say, at this point, there is only so much rush that can be built into this process. The minimum amount of time needed for the process is four hours. Therefore, it can be difficult to meet a guest's expectations when an order is not received in a timely fashion.

Training the staff makes sure that the guest's clothes aren't delayed, and that they receive the best possible service every single time. Needless to say, we dropped everything to make sure that this guest was satisfied. But it was a tricky order, because the guest was a team with their own system to make sure that everyone got the same uniforms back from the cleaners. My system adapts to the needs of the hotel and its guests, but there are times when I am amazed at how well my staff stepped in to care for the issue. Team performance was truly the winner for that team, and for the hotel staff as well.

As I mentioned previously, the hotel's binder is also the filing spot for all manifests. It makes it possible for any member of the hotel staff to find out the status of any guest order, just by going to the binder. The daily log can also be easily compared with the manifest, allowing the staff to know if an order has been returned or if it is still being processed by my facility. The manifest is also signed, so the hotel staff know who signed for the delivery, and they can be questioned right away for any potentially missing parts of the delivery.

These manifests are a critical part of my system because they give hotels and my staff a way to track orders, deliveries, and also any notes regarding the condition of the garment, from the time it entered our cleaning process until it reaches the guest again. Part of our training process is making sure that all the staff are familiar with the binder and what it offers. While being a resting place for the manifests, it is also the primary place where you can find all the procedures that make up my system.

Throughout the training process, I continually refer to the manual and binder, because I want your staff to understand how important they are to the process as a whole. If you don't know about how key they are to the system, then you might not realize what a resource the binder can be. Additionally, I want to make sure that the managers and front desk staff are familiar with the binder. This is because they are often the first individuals to deal with a disgruntled guest. By being able to reference the binder, they may be able to solve the issue for the guest in a matter of minutes. However, if they are in need of further assistance, the binder gives clear steps to follow for them to find that assistance.

The point of my system has always been to provide a service to my hotel clients, with a proven method that can be repeated time and again. Additionally, I also wanted to be able to provide a system that could be adapted by other vendors to allow them to offer outstanding service as well. For dry cleaners who might be looking to expand their business beyond the basic laundry clients, hotels can provide a great avenue to grow your business. But as my book clearly demonstrates, there are plenty of areas where you can misstep if you don't have a system in place.

My system provides a franchise option for those dry cleaners to avoid those missteps. Working with me, you can take your business to the next level by working with your local hotels to provide a value-added service that their guests will love. As I mentioned throughout these chapters, hotels are looking for a vendor that can deliver what they promise, every time. Outstanding service is key to keeping a happy hotel client. But a quality system is key to delivering that outstanding service every time.

I look forward to working with you to create the system that will move your business to the next level. No matter if you are a vendor that provides dry-cleaning or another service, be it carpet cleaning, window cleaning, or repairs, you can grow your business with hotels as your clients. Yet as you have seen throughout this book, there are key areas where vendors fail, and it ends up costing them business in the long run.

www.GoGreenOrganicCleaners.com

Key to Success: Communication

One of the key areas that I want to focus on is communication. Hotels are businesses that are constantly in motion. They need to know that their vendors will be consistent in providing their services. If a vendor misses the mark, it isn't only the vendor that loses out; it is also the hotel. Weddings, conventions, and large gatherings are often held in the hotel banquet space. This means that the hotel must use several vendors to prepare the banquet space. After all, it needs to be cleaned, the carpets shampooed and dried, tables set up, food prepared and served, as well as a myriad of other small details. Vendors are the backbone of this part of a hotel's operation. Banquet space is a critical part of a hotel's bottom line.

When a vendor is timely and communicates with the hotel about potential issues, that vendor is building a professional reputation with the hotel, which will insure repeat business. On the other hand, if the vendor is not communicating with the hotel, but instead is opting to call at the last minute to cancel—or worse yet, just not showing up—the hotel is not likely to call again. General managers have a long memory about vendors, and they are always accessing a vendor in light of their communication, their reputation, and how they have performed for the hotel in the past.

Are you looking to win back a hotel that you might not have done as well with? Then be willing to take the time to sit down with the general manager and acknowledge previous mistakes. Share with them how you have fixed those errors, and be sure to have the proof to back up your claims. They want to know that you have a system and are willing to adjust the system as needed. With the right feedback, a vendor can show a hotel, which they may have worked for in the past, that changes have been made, and that they will be able to count on you as a vendor in the future.

However, for those vendors who have not yet made the leap into the hotel business, it is key to show the hotel why they should take a chance on you and your business. What are you offering them that they haven't received from their current vendor or a previous one? Part of any sales pitch is acknowledging what you are capable of doing and how well you do it! Don't promise what you can't deliver, but when you do deliver a service or product, make it the best the hotel manager has ever seen.

Communicating effectively with your clients is the first part of providing an outstanding service. However, as you have seen throughout this book, if it isn't backed up by action, then all the communication in the world is not going to keep you on the vendor list with your hotel clients. Therefore, it is key to remember that you are representing them when you are performing a service for their hotel. Outstanding service, every time, for every guest, is their motto, and you need to feel the same when performing as a vendor for the hotel.

This chapter is about building a team between the vendor and the hotel. As a hotelier, it is also key that you are in communication with your vendors. They need to know about changes in plans, large parties booking space in the hotel, and other factors that might increase their workload. The reason is that if they know about it, they can adjust to meet those needs, or acknowledge that they can't, and work with you to find an additional vendor to deal with the overload.

Do you see how communication on both sides can have a positive or negative impact on the relationship? As vendors and hoteliers, it is a symbiotic relationship, but both sides must work together to keep it healthy. If you both perform to the others' expectations, then the relationship can last long into the future.

However, if problems do creep in, take the time to schedule a meeting to discuss it and brainstorm potential ideas to deal with the issue. You may be surprised to find that together you can create the necessary solution to reach both of your goals. Don't look at these issues as obstacles that cannot be overcome, but as challenges that can be handled. Success for both of you is a team effort.

Finally, for vendors, the reality is that hotels can always find another company to provide services to their hotel. If you want to keep your business relationships with your hotels, then you need to deliver consistently. They need to know that they can depend on you and that you will deliver outstanding services with every interaction.

When I talk with the managers of the hotels that I work with, they consistently give me the same feedback, which is they want vendors to be dependable. After all, their income stream is dependent on them fulfilling their obligations to clients, and they do so through quality vendors. Be willing to sit down with them on a regular basis, even if it is just to review your performance and make sure that you are still meeting each other's expectations.

Additionally, if you have provided outstanding service in one area, consider branching out to provide additional services to the hotels that you work with. When you have built a solid reputation, it is key to capitalize on that!

Throughout this chapter, I have focused on building a team between a vendor and a hotel. If both sides are willing to come together, it is possible that the relationship can last and be profitable to both parties!

Chapter 8

Conclusion

Throughout this book, I have explained how I created my system, how I can implement my system in your hotel, and how my team can help you to add value for your guests. The question remains, are you ready to take the leap and commit to working with me? The beauty of my system is that it is made to avoid delays in the processing of guests' garments. In fact, my system makes it easy to keep guests' garments together throughout the cleaning process; and with the manifest system, deliver them timely right to their room.

Does it mean that there are never hiccups? No, but with a system that documents each step, finding the source of the hiccup is much quicker; and often, the solution can be found in a matter of minutes, versus a longer period of time that allows a guest's anger and frustration to grow.

I believe that being available to your clients is key to providing excellent service, which is why, as part of my system, I provide you five different access numbers. That means you can always find someone who can assist you in solving any problem you might be having with a guest's order. From missing garments to unexpected damage, we can quickly solve the problem to your satisfaction, making it easy for you to provide quality service to your guests.

I understand the difficulty that working with vendors can create, just because of the lack of accountability that is often not part of their system. Why? Because many vendors do not provide a system that helps them to integrate into your hotel. As a result, they aren't making themselves a solution but another headache to manage, and a potential frustration. I want to take that frustration away from your dry-cleaning service. My team and I want to provide you first rate service with no hassle. You should be able to follow the steps of my system, and it will seamlessly work for your hotel every time.

We help hotels to implement a proven system so that their guests will receive outstanding service, and so that you are the number one provider in your local hotel industry. If you are ready to start providing that outstanding service, then contact me to move forward with creating your own system to meet any number of needs for the hotels in your area.

Recognize that if you identify a potential problem or challenge that we haven't addressed, then I am willing to sit down with you and find the solution. I believe that no system is ever perfect, but there are always methods that we can use to improve and make it better. My company is your partner, and I want to work toward your success. When you are successful, then so am I.

I understand that there are many moving parts in the running of a large hotel. From housekeeping to the front desk, there are multiple systems in place to make sure that the guest has a clean room and a great experience. Staff are trained on how to deal with guests, making sure that they feel welcome. But when a guest uses a service and they are not satisfied, it can be harder for your staff to make that guest feel as if they had a great experience.

Therefore, it is key to choose vendors that can provide consistently, while giving your staff the means to deal with any potential problems and satisfy the guest. As you have read through the previous chapters, it is clear that vendors can make or break a hotel's reputation. Most hotels will not hold onto a vendor who repeatedly makes mistakes, but for many, dry-cleaning is the service where hotels believe they must live with the errors, and that they cannot truly hold the vendor accountable. I say that hotels should be able to treat dry-cleaning like any other vendor, which means they shouldn't have unlimited chances to get it right.

I want to build a team with my hotels, because I want to help them be successful. This means I am willing to help them even in areas outside of the traditional dry-cleaning service that I provide. As a vendor, I want to go beyond just providing a service, because I want to build a long-lasting relationship. When vendors are part of the hotel's team, then they are contributing to the success of the hotel and to their own long-term success as well.

I have found that many of the hotels I work with have seen an increase in the money they are making from dry-cleaning, just because guests are more willing to use it. They see it as a reliable service and a value for them. As a vendor, it is a success that I can share with my team as our reputation grows and we are able to add more hotels to our client list.

But there are others out there who might be interested in offering a similar service to hotels in their area. If you are, I am ready to assist you in setting up your own dry-cleaning franchise, allowing you to take this system and put it in place in your area. From tagging during the pick-up process, to delivery, there are steps for every part of the process. If you are interested in franchising with me, contact me at http://www.gogreenorganics.com.

If you are a vendor who provides services to hotels, but you are having trouble creating the right system, then I can show you how to build a system that will allow you to provide high quality service every single time. Hotels want vendors who bring solutions, not problems. They want to see you as part of their team, but only if you provide a service that adds value. Working with my team, you can see the way we use a continual improvement process and different communication styles to integrate our system with every one of our clients.

No matter where you work in the hotel industry, the key is to have happy guests, because those are repeat guests. Working with the right vendors will give you the ability to have those happy guests and that value-added service, which is key to growing and building your business. So let's get started working together!

Bonus Section

During the course of my research for this book, I interviewed a variety of general managers of various hotels within the New York/New Jersey metropolitan area. What surprised me the most was how frustrating they had found previous dry-cleaning vendors, and how often they had stuck with that vendor because they didn't believe anything better was available. I showed them that better was possible with my system and the outstanding service of my team. Yet there were also some incredible insights regarding how vendors could do better in terms of improving their services for the hotels. Below are a few of the snapshots from these interviews, and a takeaway of how it can impact your business as a vendor looking to provide a service to a hotel.

The primary questions were focused on what these general managers appreciate and value in their vendors, but also about the impact of Airbnb on the hotel industry, and moments when they were able to shine for their guests.

Interview with Mark Giangiulio, General Manager of Grand Summit Hotel

What do I value or appreciate the most in my vendors? Honesty, loyalty, and professional and courteous service. I also appreciate someone who gives me a product that is consistently good. Someone that communicates with me on a timely basis if there are issues or things that we need to be concerned with. For all vendors, I also appreciate fair pricing. I mean, I don't want the cheapest, but I want the pricing to be fair, and the product to be right. Give me a good product with a good value.

In what areas can we improve, both in general and in the dry-cleaning service in particular? For dry-cleaning, we have no issues with your company. The only thing that you could do better is if you could turn it around in less than four hours, but I don't think that is possible. For other vendors, what do I think they could improve upon? I would say timeliness is a big issue in my business. When you hire a vendor to be there at 3 p.m., and they don't show up until 6 p.m., or don't show up at all, or they cancel and postpone until the next day, that is a problem for us. Now, I understand that there are circumstances that come up, but we deal with deadlines that can't be changed. We have to sell our space, and those dates are fixed.

Say for instance that we have booked a party for Thursday, and the carpet cleaning for Wednesday; that is the only day we have to do it. It has to get done on Wednesday, so when people cancel, it impacts our schedule. Timeliness is a big issue. It has happened to us before, and we had to find a new vendor.

Then, of course, the quality has to be right. You have some vendors that just don't have the quality inclination. They may think that they have quality, but the people that are actually providing the service do not have quality.

Is the Airbnb industry hurting your business now, and what do you see happening 10 years from now? Yes, it is impacting our business now. I think it will if they don't level the playing field. It will eventually be a much bigger problem for hotels. As you know, as a hotel operator, we have to follow certain rules and regulations, whether it is fire codes, safety codes, Homeland Security issues—whatever it is, we have to follow and play by the rules. We have to pay taxes, pay for inspections, and we have people coming in and out of here checking on us all the time. But if you are part of Airbnb or an Airbnb owner, and you have 10 units in Summit, then you could sell them to anybody at any time for any rate. There are no taxes, no inspections, and there are no safety precautions and other regulations. If they don't get a handle on that and level the playing field, I think it will hurt the hotel business. All you are doing is hurting people who have invested significant money into communities and businesses, hired a lot of employees, and who have followed the rules, and they are being penalized for it.

I have no problem with competition, but what needs to be done is that they need to follow the same rules as the hotels do. If I don't have customers, I still have to pay the overhead and expenses that result from these rules and regulations, which the Airbnb owner does not. I am open 24 hours a day, and Airbnb owners are not. Basically, they rent it, and that is it.

What can hotels do better in terms of service to attract more customers? I think it is to anticipate what the customer wants. To be ahead of the curve. To understand the change in the dynamics, and put things into place before the customer asks for them. To be innovative. For example, three, four, or five years ago, why weren't we the first to come up with text servicing for customers. The hotel industry should have been on top of that, but we weren't, and now it's a third party providing that. It's the same with the internet. We waited until a third-party vendor came up with the price transparency, when we should have come up with that on our own and controlled our own rate integrity.

I guess the real thing is that we need to be more aware of what is happening in people's lives, and how we can bring those things into a hotel, and provide that feeling and things they want in the hotel, before they even ask for it. I think what happens in our business is that we are playing catch-up all the time, but we need to be further ahead down the road.

It's about experiencing what they want. The customer wants certain things. There has to be a certain level of escapism when you go into a hotel, meaning that you are leaving the place that you stay all the time. When you walk in that door, there has to be a certain wow experience—somebody recognizing you, or someone greeting you in a certain way, knowing what you like to eat or drink, or what room you like, or how you like your shirts starched. To achieve that, I think you have to work your guest history. You need to understand who your customer is. You need to do research on them, build a database on them, and you need to train your people to know who these guests are when they are coming in, and how they prefer to come in. For example, Mr. Curly is here, and he has been a customer in the restaurant for perhaps 10 years, and a customer upstairs in the hotel for about 8 years. He lives down the street from the hotel. We know what he likes, so when he comes, we have certain things available for him. As a result, he keeps coming back, even though he has changed companies three different times. He keeps coming back because we know what he wants now, and we provide it for him.

Airbnb cannot provide that level of customer service. Not everyone is the same. You need to listen more, and you are not selling as hard, but you are providing services in a different way. As an industry, we have to listen more, because the customer tells us what they want.

What type of services does your hotel provide? We have everything. We have overnight sleeping accommodations; room service; lobby bar with coffee service; valet service for laundry; airport transportation; transportation services to local businesses; catering services; meeting service; off-site catering service; a restaurant that serves breakfast, lunch, and dinner; plus, we have a lounge. We have laundry services and will take care of minor sewing issues for guests if necessary. For our business customers, we offer business services, such as typing, faxing, and things like that. We will do rates for a currency exchange at Citibank in town, but we don't actually do the exchanges in house. We will arrange for people to go to different events and theaters, so we do offer concierge services as well.

What services do you feel your guests look for that you don't provide? We don't have a spa service. Well, we do, but it is not onsite; we have to send you offsite for that. Really, a big fitness center, because we just have a small room for that, and we have to send people offsite for fitness. Medical services,

How to Provide Outstanding Service to Hotels

which we do not offer, but people do ask for that, so people ask for referrals. Same with babysitting services. We do not provide that here, but people ask for recommendations. Obviously, we don't have that, for insurance and legal reasons, but we will offer people a list of individuals who can provide those types of services. Would it be profitable for us to do that? I am not so sure about this area, but maybe on weekends. The other thing is that we don't really have pet services here in the hotel. In other hotels, people carry their dogs with them wherever they go now, so they expect those services when they come to hotels.

The other service that I think would be nice to have is a bike sharing service for guests. People might like to ride bikes through town. Although we haven't done it yet, that would be very nice. These are a lot of services that local individuals provide, and we refer guests to local individuals and businesses. We can provide services, but it isn't necessarily under our roof. Because it is not here in house, it is a little different, although we do provide transportation to those services and businesses. We try to accommodate every reasonable guest request. Does every hotel do that? Absolutely not.

What do you think hotels could do to improve services to your guests? Where I think we could do the best job is to anticipate the customer's needs better. We want to know what the customer wants before they ask for it—by being able to get inside their mind without getting inside their mind; to do a better job of anticipation—that would be it.

Give me an example of a time when you have received or provided outstanding service. I did an event here last June, which was an Orthodox Jewish host wedding ceremony, and it lasted four days. It started on a Thursday and ended on a Sunday. The gentleman, who was very wealthy and shall remain nameless, basically came in and said, "I want to rent your hotel and pay everybody to leave, and utilize it for the next 96 hours. I'll pay you, and you have to provide me with this." Literally, we transformed this hotel into basically a wedding religious retreat for an Orthodox Jewish family. It was remarkable, and we were serving approximately 400 to 450 people—breakfast, lunch, and dinner, plus midnight snacks—for four straight days. It was basically 24-hour food service and non-stop 24-hour turning the rooms over and over again, and taking care of the customer. At the end of the day, the customer was blown away and couldn't believe the way we handled it. It was probably one of the more memorable service experiences that I had as a general manager, because we transformed the hotel into something it wasn't, and at the end of the day, transformed it back because we had customers coming in that night.

To do it, you have to gear up for that type of event. You aren't ready to just do it on a dime. You basically have to change the way you operate. Even toilet paper couldn't be used. We had to get the right items to accommodate the guests. You either are in it or not. I knew how to do it, so we didn't have any consultants. Do I know about it? Yes. Would I do it again? Yes. Would I do it every month? No. I would do it probably two or three times a year, when I really wanted the business, because it changes your hotel. Then you have the issue of other potential customers coming in the door; say they are coming to book a party, and they see this going on, and they don't want to see that type of thing. It's a different culture.

For instance, we have done a few Indian weddings, and I know a hotel that does a lot of them. It is a different vibe. They bring their own caterer in, and the food is set up all over the place, and the Indian catering has a different smell to it. If a potential customer sees that, they might not book their event here, because they don't feel a part of that culture. So it is a balancing act. You have to be very careful with what you do and how you do it.

An example of service gone wrong was when I had one group that didn't leave, and I had another group coming in. So I had to relocate an entire group at my expense, and put them into another hotel and pay for their meeting to occur at another hotel. Needless to say, I never booked that piece of business again. They wouldn't give me another opportunity because they were so upset. What happened was an internal error, because we overbooked the hotel, and something unforeseen happened and we were unable to accommodate both groups at the same time.

Interview with Scott McArthur, General Manager of Madison Hotel

What do you appreciate most from the vendors who provide services to you? I think what I like is people who are honest, but they are also not your typical salespeople. I don't like typical salespeople. We will call you when we need you. Don't overburden us and keep showing up, keep calling us, and keep checking in, because we have our own job to do. Those who have been successful with me and my properties are those who we get in the door, and they understand me, and I understand them. We have a professional relationship. It is not a case of every day they are trying to sell me something new or something different. They are just delivering a great product in a timely manner—what I need, when I ask for it.

With you, you made an appointment with me, and we canceled a few times; but you rescheduled versus showing up on my doorstep, interrupting my meetings and my day, or my staff's meetings and their days.

What areas do you think vendors can improve, and in particular, the dry-cleaning? Well, with you guys, it's been a year already, and you guys have been better than I anticipated, which is greatly appreciated. So really, no complaints. I know there was a situation the other day with a guest's laundry, and you took care of it quickly and professionally. You took care of it, as opposed to passing it down to somebody below. So again, having that relationship so that it goes right to the top, and somebody takes ownership of it. The problem gets resolved, and that's all I could ask for. I don't know anything about dry-cleaning, but I do know when I have unhappy customers that I have to take care of, and you meet those needs. As I said, since you have been here, there have been no complaints about the quality of work or anything. I can't worry about dry-cleaning; that's what I have you for. You seem to be meeting everybody's needs, where the previous companies weren't, and that makes me happy.

You want the vendor to be responsible for making the service run smoothly; you don't want to have to think about it. If I have to spend time on it, then it is not the service that I expect. When I hire a contractor to do a job, it means that I or my team can't do it, don't want to do it, or we don't have the time to do it. So I am bringing that person in to do a job. Just like I try to do my best at my job, and be as close to perfect as possible on my job, I want them to do that too. If I screw up, I accept responsibility for my mistakes, and I correct them. Just like that vendor, if they screw up, they need to take responsibility for their mistakes and correct them. Cause that helps all of us to do better. You got a nice piece of business from the rugby team that was here, because I feel comfortable saying, "Here, these guys will take care of you." You did, and trust me, the next place they stay, and they may not stay here, but you will be getting a call to handle their laundry.

It is good for everybody. I have a carpet cleaner that I have used for about 20 years now. He came in, and he has been very helpful and very responsive. He has gotten more business from me, because when people ask me about carpet cleaning, I tell them to use this guy. There's that honesty and trust, that he takes care of my needs, and I don't ever have to worry about it. He also comes whenever I need him, or as quickly as possible, which makes him easy for me to recommend. It is a win-win for everybody. He gets more business from doing well here, and he always takes care of me.

If you make a mistake, take ownership, and don't try to hide from it.

Do you feel that Airbnb is hurting your business now, or will do so in the future? What do you think will happen 10 years from now? No, I don't think it is hurting my business right now. Do I think that it is hurting lodging in general? I am sure there are some "mom and pops" that operate in areas in which Airbnb has taken business away. I look at them as more of a rental, like you rent a house at the beach. But I don't think it is going to hurt the hotels in the major metropolitan areas. In some aspects, like 10 years from now, I think it is going to be just like it is today. It's a fact, just like Uber. It is the same situation. It is something new, something cool, and people are doing it. Some places will be really good, and other places won't be good. You see some of the problems with it, where people have been hurt by Uber drivers, and people have driven with Uber drivers that were drunk, or this or that. So at least with name-brand, big independent hotels, you know there is going to be a level of consistency and a level of trust. You stay at this hotel, and it's been here for 60 years, so you know that this is what you are going to get. It's on Trip Advisor. The same is true if you stay at a Hilton or a Marriott; you know what you are getting. With Airbnb, if you go on their sites, you just don't know what you are getting. My assistant will tell you how he was going somewhere and thought he was getting one price, and as it got closer, the price changed, and the pictures changed. He wasn't getting what he thought he was getting. That will happen a few times, and I think it will lose some of its luster. But again, if you go down to the beach or the Jersey shore, people are always looking for a bargain. There is a market for that.

I think there will be a market for it, but do I think it is going to hurt our business? With my property in this area, no, I don't think so.

How do you think you could improve service for your guests if money and resources were not an issue? At this particular property, I wouldn't change the look of it. I think it is our marketing niche and who we are. There are capital things that I would like to do, and eventually we will. I would like to get a bigger fitness center. I would also like to do some renovations. Same look and quality of product, but newer products. Service itself, I feel very comfortable with our team. Most of us have been here a long time, and we have had very little turnover. When we took over, we were ranked last in our area on Trip Advisor. Now we are not only first on Trip Advisor for our area, but we have been for five straight years. And we are number one in all of Morris County out of 52 hotels. We can always do better, but I don't think it is a money or capital issue; I think it is about having the right people, who are always going to be positive. It will never happen 100 percent of the time. Chris and I have to keep it upbeat and up tempo, and always friendly, no matter what is going on in our lives.

I think it is just a case of myself and my management team working to keep our team motivated to provide great service all the time, as much as possible. I don't think it is a money or resource issue; I think it is about my team and that we keep pushing them to smile and greet guests. I think we have a great product here, other than improving through renovations and getting newer stuff, brighter stuff. I feel pretty good about where we are. Customers respond to a good attitude, and attitude is what it is all about.

You and I are the same. We manage people, and we have to deal with everything that goes on in people's lives, good, bad, or indifferent. In our role, at times, we have to step up and say, "You know what, you can't be at the front desk tonight. Your head just isn't in the game. Go to the back of the house and do something out of the public eye, and get your head back in it." Things happen, and we have to be able to step up and step in, to fill that role while they get their heads straightened out. It's not a case where we are threatening people with job loss; we aren't terminating people, and we aren't even necessarily coaching or counseling people. It is more of a pat on the back, a smile, and saying, "Keep your chin up. I know it is tough out there." We have to take care of our customers. But I am pretty happy with the people we have now.

Did you ever receive training on how to handle guest and employee clothes? Do you think it could be valuable to provide training in that area? I did receive that training, but only because, in the early 1980s, I worked in a hotel that did their own dry-cleaning. I think where my team has been successful, and where I have been successful, is that I have always tried to reduce everything to the lowest common denominator; the easiest and most simplistic way possible. I break it down to the basics and build it up from there, almost like the military, particularly the way the Marines do it. They terrorize you through basic training; they break you down and make you cry and make you hurt. But when you come out, you are tough, efficient, and professional. I think that it is the same thing here.

We have been successful, and my teams have been successful, because I like for them to know everything about running a hotel, but I want them to really focus on what is most important, which is taking care of the customer that is in front of them at the time. Me, personally, I wouldn't have my team learn about that, because there is going to be a very rare, rare, rare chance that someone would ask them a question, or that it would become beneficial to them to learn something like that. I would rather have them learning computers, coming up with new ways to improve customer service at the hotel, or to add a new amenity, or subtract one that is wasting time or resources, than worry about things that they really can't control. Because they can't control how good of a dry cleaner you are. They can't control the product that is delivered. They can tell you that it doesn't look good and that it doesn't smell good, but they can't actually go there and touch it or feel it and make it better.

I like to focus on things that they can touch, feel, and make better, because I know they are invested in it. I know, with me, it is the same thing. If I can't give 100 percent to it, or I can't promise myself that I can deliver a product 100 percent, I usually pass that by. If somebody else can mess it up for me, and my name is on it, I don't want my name on it. I don't want to put my name on something that I can't personally carry through to the end and deliver. I would rather have my team focus on the things that they can control and that they can really make their own and take ownership of.

What other types of services does your hotel provide? Well, we have the two restaurants. We have catering. Obviously, we have ancillary services, such as shuttle driving, internet, Wi-Fi service, television, and telephone services—things like that. It could be the same as in most large hotels.

Have you talked about adding some services that you do not currently provide? Well, we offer the shuttle service that will take them to a variety of services, up to a five-mile radius. This lets them take advantage of other amenities in our local area.

What types of services are guests looking for that you do not provide? There is nothing. With today's technology, with the internet and social media, people know exactly or almost exactly what they are getting when they come here. They know that they are going to a limited service property, like a Hampton Inn or a Red Roof Inn. They know that when they come here, they are going to have parking, shuttle service, television service, room service, and two food service outlet choices. They can choose either fine dining or a pub atmosphere. We have catering and meeting services. It is all out there for the world to see. Those who don't have the internet, they call, and our staff is trained to answer their questions. We have a menu, per se, of things that people ask questions about. It allows our staff to say that this is what we have here, and here is what we offer. All of our front desk staff is trained on that and making proper reservations. Included when they do those reservations, and they have test calls, they have to mention three things that our hotel offers. So whoever is thinking of making a reservation knows at least the minimum of three things that our hotel offers. This way, guests know what they are getting right from the start.

That is my biggest frustration, when I read something on Trip Advisor and they say negative things about our hotel, but there are thousands of pictures everywhere. Some people come in and seem surprised, but how can you be surprised in this day and age? If anything, I would want to be able to say, "Here's what you are getting, here is what it looks like, cancel before you get here if you are disappointed, so you aren't upset," kind of things.

I think that was one of my missions as an independent from my brand days. When I first took over this hotel, I had to rebrand the entire thing. Our key cards had a picture of our hotel on the front. Everything we have, including our guest of the day prizes, has our logos on them and our websites. It might be a drinking glass, a coffee mug, or a thermal mug, or comment cards, letterhead, website, and sales kits—I rebranded everything. Even if you look at our business center, the cover screen is a picture of our hotel. It is basically about putting our brand out there and letting people know that this is who we are. When you go to a Hilton, you know what you are getting. When you go to a Marriott, you know what you are getting.

That was my idea. When we first opened, we went to many businesses and handed out little gifts with our logos on them, and then we encouraged people to go to our website, and encouraged them to go to Trip Advisor, so that they could see the pictures and see what we have. Now that we have marketed and we are doing all these social media things, I don't think people are too surprised by what they get. I think we compete pretty well with the chain hotel properties. My background is in luxury hotel service, and when I came here, that is what I wanted to do. How much could we do with the staff we had so that people coming here could have everything that they wanted? I think for the most part, we have met that goal. The question is, do people get our concept, because we are different.

The way we look is different, and some people get it and some people don't. That is the one thing that I can't sell. If you don't like our style, I can't change your mind, and there is nothing that I can do about that. But I still kill you with kindness and good service. I can provide you with a nice clean product, so at least when you are here, you might not like the décor, but the staff will treat you well and give you great service, and it will be nice, clean, and well maintained. We sell cleanliness, service, and security. That is what we sell. That is what I focus on, not how we look.

Branding and marketing are number one. Your brand provides a unique experience that makes you stand out from all the hotels in your area.

Can you give an example of when you received or gave outstanding service? In my role, I have multiple bosses besides the customers; I have the ownership group, the management company I work for, and my team itself. So, in my role, I look at things differently than I did before I became a GM. I think I provide outstanding service to my owners, because again, when we took over, occupancy was very low, and revenue was very low. In three years, we doubled revenue, and occupancy rose from below 40 percent to above 70 percent. Every financial indicator found in the hotel industry, for this hotel, has improved year after year after year, which is good for my ownership group and is also good for my management group. The company is paid based on how much revenue we bring in. So in my role, where I provided outstanding service was that I put together a team and took a product and fine-tuned it. It keeps guests coming back for the product and also the service. The building has been well-maintained. Therefore, more money is flowing to the bottom line because there is less money going out for expenses in fixing things and repairs. That is where I am.

If you talked about way back when, I worked for a hotel and we had a guest fly in for a big interview, and he had forgotten his shoes. I asked him what size he was, and I gave him my shoes because he was my size—and I walked home in a blizzard. I lived about a block and a half away, so I had to walk in my sock feet in the snow. The customer wrote a letter, and it made it up the hierarchy. I have known my team to go pick up items for customers. One held a customer's head while they were sick, and gave them ginger ale to help them feel better. Making calls for them because they can't, because they don't feel well; ironing, sewing, and tons of other things for guests; our night front desk staff just sitting and listening to people who are lonely, taking the time to just listen and let our guests talk—those are the things that I love. If I see an employee having a conversation with a guest about something personal, I will step in and do their job, just so they don't have to interrupt that interaction. People feel at home here, and that's what we want.

Give me an example of when you have provided bad service. I am somewhat of a perfectionist and, at times, I think I am not as compassionate as I could be. People are having a bad day, or they are frustrated and they write a bad letter or something else, and I stand there and listen, thinking to myself, "You just don't get it." Instead of me being empathic, in my head I have already admitted defeat, and I keep telling myself that there is nothing I can do to help them get it. I usually am thinking to myself, "Stop complaining." Admittedly, I could be better about that. You know, I have to understand that people need to speak, people need to vent, and if I think it is valid, I will listen forever. If I don't think it is valid, I will shut them down too soon, or they can see it in my face and body language that I am shutting them down. That is something that I have done on occasion, and something that I have to get better about.

Interview with Lee Trilling, General Manager of Westin Hotel

What do you appreciate most from the vendors who provide services to you? What I appreciate most is follow-up and follow-through. It is very important. A lot of times, you will get a vendor that forgets who the client is. Very recently, just two weeks ago, there was a vendor, and we were talking about what my expectations were, and he disagreed with me about what I wanted, which just blew my mind. So it is listening to what the client's needs are, and in your world, it's not my client, it is *our* client. They referred to the people that we forward to them for business, as my client, and I had to correct them. Our vendor, or I like to refer to them as our partner, doesn't recognize that it is a joint venture. We both have an interest in succeeding, and if they don't get that, then it is just not going to work. Follow up and follow through, and understand that it's a partnership for both of the entities' success.

In what areas do you think we can improve in general, and in the area of dry-cleaning in particular? I am very happy. I have been in this market and dealing with the industry for a long period. As I said to you, as an operator, the less you hear from me, the better. And I would say that I never have to call you, except for something personal or I need assistance on something unique. Overall, I am very pleased with how you are handling it, based on our volume, for both my external guests and my internal guests; and with the way we don't have things get lost, but if they are misfiled or misplaced, there is a quick turnaround, and it is almost immediately resolved. I have dealt with other dry cleaners or partners, and when things go awry, they don't take ownership. Not with you, but with some of your competitors in the market. What they will say is, "It wasn't us, it was you," or "It wasn't us, it was them," rather than saying, "Even though I am right, this is the cost of doing business, and I need to make it right." I will track it and bring it to Lee, and saying it doesn't make sense, is a problem. But with the one-offs, let's not chase pennies; let's just fix it.

I mean, why am I, as the general manager, having to get involved and make a call, saying, "Guys, it's $30. Just waive it, and you will make it up in volume." Time and time again, that is an issue. If it is your fault, just pay for it and move on.

Another thing, not with you, is that other dry cleaners do not change their chemicals as often, so it builds up an odor. They might be changing them for the regular clients, but for the in-house clients, they might not be changing them as frequently. Then I have complaints from the staff that because they are free or discounted, we aren't getting treated as well. It shouldn't be that way. You have to treat every client as if they are the general manager, and they should get the same results.

Is Airbnb hurting your business right now, and what do you think will happen in 10 years? If we were a destination location, it would be hurting our business for sure. But we are not a destination location, and we are not a resort. We are not in an area where people go because we are by an academy or by a school or whatever, so it doesn't impact us because most of our clients during the week are corporate clients who are here for business, and they want the points for their stay, and they like the brand loyalty. I could see it if we were in New York or Hoboken; a different story, because those are destinations where people like to nickel and dime. Where we are, we aren't seeing it. In other markets, however, it is impacting business greatly, because you can get a Airbnb for $100, where your rate could be $200. It certainly is a factor you have to pay attention to in those markets. It is similar to Uber, because you are taking a risk. If you get hurt, you are on your own. If there is an incident, or you cause an incident, you are on your own. You are not protected. If you were to stay in a Airbnb, and a fire should break out, then you could be held personally libel. Whereas if you are here, it only gets to a certain point before our coverages would come in and take care of it, from a safety factor and general liability, because you don't know what they have. Wherever I would spend my money, you would have to treat it that someone would feel safe bringing their kids there. I personally don't think our market overall has the same comfort level as a branded hotel. The same thing with a car service. Even though I think the taxi cab industry is crazy, I feel better with my daughter going in a yellow cab than in an Uber cab. They are more professional, insured, and they are vetted better. Even though I think they are crazy too, if I had a choice between a yellow cab and a private car, I don't know who that guy is in the private car, and I don't have a license number. They are not registered, and I don't know if they have insurance. So I would treat the Airbnb the same way.

In the next 10 years, I think both those areas are going to get regulated. At some point, Airbnb has more of a challenge than an Uber company, because there are more regulations when it comes to dealing with the boards and bylaws like that. You see the way that they have been getting away with it now; they are circumventing that by sneaking them in, rather than letting them come in through the front door. The more it becomes obvious, the more challenges will present themselves. I don't see Airbnb being as successful as Uber; I really don't.

If money or resources were not an issue, how would improve service to your guests? I would run it like a five-star resort. If I had endless resources, I would run it like the Plaza in New York City, or the Waldorf Astoria, where it is 24-hour service with 24-hour staff. Unfortunately, in these elements, it is not profitable to run a 5-diamond hotel. They are becoming more and more rare. But that is the perfect scenario, to have all your operations going 24 hours. Right now, if you walked in, my bellman's not there. It is because the revenues do not afford me the ability to have multiple bellmen.

Certain services, based on your business levels, aren't justified. But if there were endless resources, you certainly wouldn't have to worry about that. For example, as a chain, we have to have 24-hour food service. Does that mean that my kitchen is open 24 hours a day to bring a hot meal up at 3 in the morning? No, the offering changes, because my kitchen is closed; the late-night offerings are cold offerings instead. So the service is impacted by that.

Does any company come and train your staff on the dry-cleaning business, and would it be useful, such as how to handle guests' clothes? No, they don't. They give you a general understanding of how to manage the service, and typically that goes based on experience. In the hotels I have been, only one has had dry-cleaning in house. So, basically, through the years, I learned how to manage that service. Early on, it was being mentored by my predecessors, and it has evolved. So everyone has a different way, and it gets tweaked and fine-tuned, until it becomes the standard. That is what happens with most standards in hotels—everybody contributes. At any given point, my management (which is from a variety of hotels and backgrounds) come together and say, "Well, I did it this way," and someone else says, "I did it that way." You merge all those ideas and policies into place, and that becomes your standard. That's how I believe it has evolved.

You have your different properties managed by different operators, but it is almost always the same playbook. Everyone is using the same playbook, and it is because it has evolved over the years as individuals experimented and evolved through their careers.

Typically, when I get a new vendor, they have a meeting with the front desk staff and the housekeeping staff, and they find out how they do it and then explain their process, and they decide which way is going to work best for the hotel, and that is how they proceed. So I think that is definitely important as you take on new accounts, but no one from the corporate office would come in and talk about it. You don't know what you don't know.

What other types of services does your hotel provide? We have full food service and room service. We also offer Westin Lending Gear. Most people don't like to check their luggage, so they have this small luggage. So our brand came up with this idea. Our brand is Bell Wellness, Eating Well and Being Well. So they said that we are going to have sneakers and workout clothes available at the hotel; and for a minimal fee, we will provide this service so that they don't have to take up that space in their suitcase. So they come, and the shirt and the pants are free with the service, and if they use the sneakers, it's $5. If they like the equipment and they buy it, then you make a little money. But that is something that is very unique.

We have a shoeshine service. We have what used to be our business center, which was a huge profit because we made copies and offered a variety of services, but now that everyone is mobile, that service has been dissolved. It is almost a little kiosk now, whereas before you might have had a big desk. We have the shuttle service, and then we have those additional services you would get, such as turndown service and other amenities. We also have the pool and catering events. We do an equal amount of revenue with our catering that we do with our hotel. It is very rare, because usually catering is about 1/3 of your business, and this is half. The budget is big, as big as some budgets for a whole hotel. Sometimes guest rooms were related to the events, but that was a very small percentage.

Would you like to have some other services that you do not currently provide? We are different from independent hotels because we are a branded hotel, and we cannot deviate from the brand. If we were to provide a service, it would have to be a branded service, and that is the only caveat. For example, before Dolce became Wyndham, they had the freedom to do that, and they offered a variety of different services. Now Starwood or Wyndham will come in and audit you, and if they see something there, then it could be a problem. We have a spa, but we treat the spa as independent, not branded as Westin. If we were to brand it as Westin, then we would have to follow their standards, procedures, and policies. So we treat it just like the restaurant; it is a separate entity from Westin. We are allowed to have the spa; it's just that it cannot be branded as part of Westin in any way except that it is under this roof.

Using vendors allows us to offer services with professionals performing the service. Like for example, could I do dry-cleaning? No, but could I attempt it? Yeah, but would the results be the same? Probably not. It's the same thing. You know what you are good at. I could provide a variety of services, but they wouldn't be as good, and the extra money I would make wouldn't be worth it.

What areas does your hotel excel in? Our food and beverage program is better than anybody else. We have fine dining. Our dining experience is one of the few in the state of New Jersey that offers fine dining solutions. Fine dining is very high-end food cuisine, and very unique cuisine, such as farm to table. Instead of buying it from the mass market, we have partners in the local community that provide us what we need. With most hotels, their food program is mandated by the corporate office, and you have no creativity, and it is not defined as part of the fine dining cuisine. That carries through to our catering. Because we get the creativity and the vision, that carries through to our catering services.

We manage the restaurant. It is our entity, but it is separate from the hotel itself. It is not a Westin, but it is ours. Westin is good at providing a great home away from home solution, and meeting the needs of today's travelers, but you have to know when you need to partner. Do what you are great at. Concentrate on your strengths, not your weaknesses. You can partner for what you need support with.

Give me an example when you received or provided outstanding service. We had an event here. Now, individuals will come to the area for a specific event, and we will create a room block for that event. We had a room block for a wedding, but the event itself was being held at another venue. But we got hit with a major snowstorm, and it shut down the whole state. They couldn't get to their venue, so we had their wedding here with the staff that we had, and it was very successful. There were no surcharges or upcharges; we just wanted to do the right thing for them. We received recognition for that.

Everyone asked why we would do that without getting any extra money for it. It was because, out of the 300 people there, everybody knew what we did, and now we are a staple. We immediately got 5 pieces of business out of it, and it continues to grow just based on that word of mouth. And I specifically asked that it not be publicized, because I didn't want to make it public knowledge in that I didn't want it to feel that we did it just to get PR. We did it because it was the right thing to do. We got the business anyway. We got the PR, but we didn't do it based on only doing it if they put us in the newspaper, or if they got us a certain amount of business. We did it knowing that we were going to get the business anyway, because we weren't going to be secretive about it. But if we leveraged it based on that, it wouldn't have been real. It wouldn't have been organically done, and it would have looked like we were fake and had alternative motives.

By partnering with somebody when it is the right thing to do, you will always benefit down the road financially. But if you try to force it, then it will never come to fruition.

Give me an example when you have received or provided a bad service. When we didn't learn from our mistakes. Just in general, we have many opportunities to capture clients' feedback, and if you don't notice where you have the defects, and fix the defects, you are never going to learn from it. Like if a guest comes in and says that they didn't like the food and the room type. If you don't capture that guest's information, then they are going to come and experience the same thing. You are going to put them in the wrong room, and you are going to cook their steak the wrong way. If you don't capture what the scenarios were, and find the pattern and learn from it, then that is the biggest mistake. As tough as it is to hear it, if you never learn from it, then you will never succeed.

If you sit there and don't look yourself in the mirror and be honest with yourself and your team, you are going to fail. Have the ability to listen and hear what your shortcomings are, and correct them; if you don't do that, it is the biggest failure that you can ever have.

What stands out to me is when a vendor brings something to my attention. Like if you bring in my dry-cleaning and tell me that I "had a loose button, just so you know, but it is on us." Or if you did that for a guest, and told them to let you know if they would like you to fix it. If you did that, it would really be the extra bump of customer service. When you do something like that, it not only looks good on you, it looks good for me, because they see that we partnered together and you went the extra mile.

Interview with Kevin Catrambon, General Manager Hilton Garden Inn

What do you appreciate most from the vendors that provide services for you? I appreciate the most from vendors when they have an understanding of service and the expectation of service. One, the level of service that we want to provide to our guests, and the understanding of the service and the urgency to provide a service. I understand that operational challenges are going to arise, but how do we recover from those challenges that make a difference to me and that make a difference to our guests? We want to be treated like your customers, just as we want to treat our customers with value. I want you to understand how we want our customers treated, because then you will treat them the same.

In what areas do you think vendors can improve in general, and in dry cleaning in particular? I think the reason we selected you was that you already know what we want to provide to our guests, so you provide them with consistency. You provide them with reliability. You provide them with pretty much everything that you need to right now, from pricing to everything. You have been very flexible, allowing us to offer your services to our guests. So I think you are really providing them with everything that they need at the moment. I don't think there is anything more that you need to provide them. I just hope that you continue to provide them with consistency and a quality product, which I am sure that you will.

Is Airbnb hurting your business now, and what do you think will happen in 10 years? Airbnb is certainly showing an impact in some of the areas, New York being one of them, where they are taking a share from the hotels. But there are 700 hotels in New York, and more to come. I think it is just another piece of the pie that is being taken away from the hotels. It is just a lot of supply in the area. I think one thing they will find with Airbnb is that they won't find a consistent quality product. You pretty much don't know what to expect.

To me, I would have a hard time selecting it going away with my family, because I would be concerned about the location, the safety, and sharing an apartment with people. But I guess it is the same as taking an Uber. You take your chances choosing between an Airbnb or booking a hotel, and you take a chance choosing between a licensed taxi driver and an Uber driver. I guess you can take a chance with everything, but for me, I would go for the consistent product, where I know that they are going to deliver, and I know what to expect.

I don't think someone booking at one of the Hilton family hotels is going to look for an Airbnb. If they were going to look for an Airbnb, they probably wouldn't be booking the Hilton brand hotels; they might be booking a different type of hotel.

If money and resources were not an issue, how do you envision improving service to your guests? I would provide more of an ambassador-type journey. Somebody, or two or three people, would handle everything for the guests—above and beyond a sleeping room, above and beyond breakfast, above and beyond Broadway tickets. We are going to create their journey for them, from before they get here to the time, we get them back home. So to me, I would be able to have a service that was available for someone to say, "Book my trip; this is what I want to do while I am there," and they would walk in the door, and we would hand them their itinerary with their tickets and the car service set up. We would have everything they need from the minute that they walk in the door, to the minute they walk out the door.

It is probably doable. It is a couple of more people on the payroll. It will get us repeat business, but I am still going to have to charge the same, so it is not going to get me the return on investment. That is more futuristic, because it is going to be down the road for me, in the form of people returning. I don't know how much value it would have for us. A guest would probably see it as a great value, but how much they would be willing to pay is another thing.

Does your management company do or offer comprehensive training in addition to those from the companies, like Hampton and Hilton? Both. Our management company, Hersha Hospitality Management (HHM), provides us with a lot of resources and training. Whether it is online training, classroom training, or general conferences, they are always looking to develop our team members. We have a couple of programs in place right now, where we select secondary level managers that we say are going to be future leaders at HHM, and send them to a special course. They go to a special course to continuously and further develop their skills as managers, so that they can then take over and be the future leaders of our company. Then there is training from the brands. So there are seminars and caucuses, and some are in general sessions and online training. So training is always available to us; it is just a matter of who wraps their arms around it.

There is training that goes all year long, whether it is webinars or conferences. You can go to as many as you like or as few as you like. There are a few mandatory ones, but at the same time, there are so many courses, like a college. We have Hilton University, where I can log on at any time and take any training that I want. HHM has the same program; it's called Empower Me, and you can go on and take any courses that you want, to really develop yourself and keep fresh.

Do you ever get trained on how to handle guest and employee clothes, or do you think it would be valuable to give that training? No, we don't get training in it. I think it is important for us to know, when you look at this laundry slip for dry cleaning, what's on it. There are so many things on it: do you want it folded, do you want it hung, do you want it starched or not starched? Most of our guests who use the dry cleaning service are trained in what they want, but our staff is not, unless they use dry cleaning services themselves. Chances are they are doing their own clothes, so they might not know what all of that stuff means. I would think that a concierge's service would need to know if you had a concierge's station in the hotel. It would probably be helpful for them to be versed on it, and possibly have a 10-minute course on what it is and what the items mean—things like what starch does, and what heavy starch is, or what types of stains can be removed. What is express service, and what is involved as far as time frames? I think it could be an online training or even a disk that they can pop in and follow.

I think you also need to get out of the guests' minds. People come to hotels and they probably don't think that they are going to get their clothes dry cleaned there. Most people don't get it paid for when they are traveling, and most people think it is outrageous, like you don't make phone calls in the hotel, and everybody knows that because it is expensive. I think they have the same mindset for dry cleaning, and you probably want to get them out of that mindset, to the one where we are just here to provide a service and not to make money. Of course, everyone wants to make money, but I don't want them to think that we are trying to make money on the service. We just want them to realize we are trying to provide a service. How do you do that? It starts with volume.

What other types of services does your hotel provide? We have a restaurant. We have guest laundry on the 7th floor, which is a coin-operated washer and dryer. We have complimentary internet and upgraded internet for a cost. We do coffee service in the morning. We are part of the Hilton family, so you gain points and credits for your stay. We have a great location. I think we are close to everything, yet far enough away from the craziest parts of the tourist areas.

In what area does your hotel excel at or provide exceptional service? Our motto is to create an experience for each guest that comes through the door, instead of just providing them with a stay. Every hotel is going to give you a bed, a coffee maker, an iron, and a bathroom. We are going to give you the same, but we are going to create more of a memory for them. We want to personalize the service for them. We want to know who they are, and what their likes and dislikes are. Are they celebrating a birthday? What can we do? Did they not have a great trip in? What can we do to brighten their day? Are they not feeling well? Can we send soup to their room?

Making a difference and standing out as a hotel, but more of a comfort zone for them, where we make them feel welcome as opposed to "here is your bed, here is your key," and then moving on.

Can you give me an example of when you received or provided outstanding service? It is such a natural instinct to me to provide quality service that I don't see it as an outstanding task.

Can you give me an example of when you received or provided bad service? I tend to provide bad service when people are disrespectful to me. I don't expect people to come in and scream and yell at my team. We are not here to be yelled at. So, when they are screaming, cursing, and yelling at my team members, I tend to step in, and I don't necessarily provide the best service. Most of the time, I will just cancel their reservation and ask them to leave, because they are obviously not the type that I want staying at the hotel, or would feel comfortable with them speaking to my team that way. That is when I would step in and probably not provide the best service.

Interview with Keith Moses, General Manager of Hilton Complex

What do you appreciate most from the vendors that provide services for you? Those that provide a superior level of service to all of our guests. My expectation as a general manager is exactly the same for all my vendors. I don't want to have to worry about the execution side of it from my vendors. I choose my vendors wisely, either through relationships or past experiences. There is a certain level of trust that I adhere to with these vendors, to make sure they are providing the same level of service to me as they are to my guests. At the end of the day, the guest doesn't matter, because no matter what service is provided, it is me that they are holding accountable for it. So, my expectation for my vendors is no different than if it were me executing for my guests.

What areas do you think vendors can improve in general, and dry cleaning in particular? I would say the knowledge of allergies. In this day and age, people have a lot of allergies. I don't know much about the dry cleaning business. As a general manager, knowledge is absolutely critical. If someone has an allergy, and someone comes down and asks what specific chemicals you use, I would like to have that knowledge and be able to provide them that knowledge. I think more information provides me the ability to provide a better service to our customers. You may not be able to do it because you use certain chemicals, but I may have another vendor that can do it. Knowledge, as a general manager, is important, because our guests are relying on us, especially with the large amount of international travelers that we have. They come over here, and they rely on the big brand hotels to be able to provide these services to them. The more knowledge you can provide us, be it dry cleaning or any other service, or just the general information about the business, the more I can speak intelligently to our guests.

Is Airbnb hurting your business now, and what do you see happening 10 years down the road? I think Airbnb is very specific to a very specific type of traveler. It is a great idea and a great concept, but I think those that are staying with us are very loyal and loyal to the brand. Airbnb offers those that are looking for that type of experience, and I truly believe that we are a very different experience here. At our hotel specifically, we have all the great amenities that you would expect at a Hilton, and we provide all the services of a full-service Hilton as well. Again, while I think Airbnb is a great concept, I think it is geared to a specific traveler, a customer that is looking for those types of accommodations and those types of services. Again, I don't think there is any immediate impact on us in the future.

If money and resources were not an issue, how would you improve service to your guests? Training is the heartbeat of every hotel. You could have all the associates you need, but at the end of the day, if they are not the right associates, it really doesn't make a difference. I really think the more training you can provide, the more power you provide your associates to make good decisions, and educate them on how to provide superior service. Because at the end of the day, we can hire great people with great technical skills, but you can't ask them to smile. Again, I think through good training and a good work environment, those things stem to a great performance. At the end of the day, if I had unlimited funds to invest into our associates, that's how I believe you are really going to make a difference in the end. Every hotel has an infrastructure and has four walls, bedrooms, pools, and restaurants. But what makes us unique is the experience our associates provide to the customers. So, I truly believe if you can make a large enough investment, with unlimited funding, I think training is the best way to go.

Have you ever been trained on how to handle guest and employee clothes, and do you think that type of training is needed or would be valuable? No, I think if the information is passed on to me as the general manager, I would pass it on to our associates. I would go through the information and determine what I thought they truly needed to have, because I think that could be a little overwhelming for them, and I want to keep them focused on providing great service.

What other kinds of services does your hotel provide? Other than the experience itself, we have the overnight experience, which includes the room they sleep in; different restaurant offerings, whether it is the breakfast, lunch, or dinner experience; and the pool and all the great amenities, including the fitness center. But if you are talking strictly from the service point of view, the service we provide that brings the most benefit to our guests is the shuttle service, because the shuttle service can get those guests off property that may have been here for one or two weeks, who want to try something different or taste something different. We have shuttle service to various attractions in the area. Our shuttle service runs within a three-mile radius, including to some businesses that we have a relationship with. Again, if they need to go to FedEx to make some copies or pick up office supplies, or go to Walmart and pick up some groceries, or they need to run to a restaurant in the local area, we can certainly take them within a 3-mile radius, but that is just a nice added benefit that we can offer to our guests, especially those who are here for a long period of time.

In addition to that, we have the washer and dryer services that are right here on the property, which we have for people who are here for sports events or an extended period of time. That way they don't need to be running off property or to and from the property just for regular washer/dryer services.

What do you think guests look for that you don't provide? I think we provide all the services one would be looking for when they are staying in a hotel. The one thing about being a hotelier, and this has been true a long time, is that if we can't provide a service, we will find that service and bring it to us, for the guests. That is how we are brought up; it is in our DNA. If we don't have it here, we will find a way to bring it here; and if we can't, then there is a good reason why we can't. I think the unique requests we get can be met most of the time. In our fitness center, we have a lot of cardio equipment and free weights. But we don't have a universal piece of equipment in there. So it is important for me to understand that the specific equipment a guest may want, and be used to, might not be available, and it is also important for me to have a relationship with a local gym in the area, so that I can say, "I don't have it here, but I have a great shuttle service that can take you to that gym, so that you can use that equipment."

It's the same thing with our gift shop. We aren't going to carry everything that a convenience store carries. We have a lot of things that a business or leisure traveler might need, but there might be something in there that I don't have. But again, I have that shuttle service, or I can run out and get it for that guest, or I can take that guest to the supermarket to pick those up. There really aren't any requests that we can't honor.

Give me an example of when you have received or provided outstanding service. I hope it is every day. Being in my position, I would like to acknowledge the associates that do it every day. Truly they do. They go out of their way, and that is the expectation and standard that I set as the general manager. From the top down, it is important that I do the same things on a day-to-day basis, and that is certainly making sure that I am interacting with my guests as frequently as I can, so our associates can see that, and it becomes contagious. One specific example that I remember is when we had a group staying in the hotel with us, and they were international travelers. It was a group of kids traveling with passports. When you are traveling internationally as students, you tend to take your valuables and you lock them up. We provide the safety deposit boxes for our guests to do so. For some reason, there was something that was left behind in the back office, before they left to get on a plane and go home. I made it a point to make sure that I followed our extended protocol, but when they called me, I got on a train and made sure that they got their belongings before they got on the plane and headed at home. The expectation would be no different for me than any other associate, to make the experience memorable. I know that the next time they travel here, they will choose the hotel that I am at, because they will remember the service that I provided. It is that important. Again, every hotel is just bricks and mortar, and we all have rooms and pools, but what they don't always have is people like the associates within those four walls that make the difference.

Give me an example of when you have provided or received bad service. I hope we never provide bad service, because that is not the business that we are in. Anybody can make mistakes, but it is how you recover from those mistakes that makes the difference. Again, there are going to be times when a guest is not going to be 100% satisfied with the actions that we may provide, but it is the recovery that makes the difference. We all make mistakes, but that interaction that they have with me, or with the restaurant server or the front desk agent, will make the difference of whether or not that guest comes back or not. So again, from a bad service standpoint, it is difficult for me to say, but I truly in my heart believe that when everybody leaves the hotel, we did everything in our power to make sure that we recognized that mistake, and that we made a decision to make it right before they left. And that is really the motto in this building—guests do not leave unhappy—because it is very important that we retain all of our guests, or at least try to bring them back each and every time.

Interview with Jim Hecox, General Manager of a Best Western

What do you appreciate most from the vendors that provide services for you? We have vendors of all kinds. I appreciate when vendors, especially when they are providing products versus a service, provide the ability to return products quickly and easily without any hassle at all. Similar to a customer, they want to be able to return an item to the store quickly and easily. Costco and Macy's are good examples of that. So, they tend to get more buys that way. I like vendors like that. The service-oriented ones, I just want them to come in with a fair price, and come in and do their service, almost as if they are not seen or heard or anything. It works out well then.

What areas do you think vendors can improve in general, and dry cleaning in particular? With dry cleaning, I don't know if you can provide any better service. You do an excellent job. It is set up so that if we have laundry going out, we call you, and you pick it up and return it the same day. We have never had anything lost. We have never had anything missing. I don't think we have even had any damage. So I don't think there is anything you can do better in regard to dry cleaning. That's exactly what we are looking for.

Is Airbnb hurting your business now, and what do you see happening 10 years down the road? I don't think Airbnb is hurting us now. I think they are hurting hotels in bigger cities, like New York or Chicago. I don't think they are really hurting our market yet, but I think it is coming. The reason I say that is because we are very much a corporate hotel, and I don't think businesses are using Airbnb to the fullest extent yet. I have a funny feeling that this will switch in the next five years or so, and once that starts switching, then we will have some trouble. Hopefully by then, the government has their act together and is taxing them and regulating Airbnb units as they do hotels. Then at least we are playing on a level playing field. It is similar to Uber. They aren't taxed or regulated either, and it's the same for us as the taxi industry. So, I think if you can get them both on a level playing field, we will be okay. They can charge less because they do not have the overhead that we do.

For me, it's not so much about the staffing overhead though, because I think that is a plus that they don't have. It's the taxes. We have to charge a 15% sales tax, and they aren't charging anything. We just aren't on a level playing field. They are also not being inspected by anybody. We are inspected by the state, and have fire inspections. We have liability and umbrella insurance; they do not have insurance. Additionally, those services that we can provide are a plus. The people that we have are basically concierges, whereas at Airbnb, you aren't getting anything.

If money and resources were not an issue, how would you improve service to your guests? Hiring more people, because the more people you have, the better service you can provide to everybody. We go a lot of shifts on our front desk with one person, so if they are on the phone, and somebody walks in to be checked in, or somebody comes up to ask a question, they have to wait. If I had more people, they wouldn't have to wait. If money wasn't an issue, that is what I would do.

Does your management company do the training, or do you receive training from the different brands? We actually just manage Best Westerns; we have three of them. Our training actually comes from both. We do in-house corporate management training, which means that the corporate office is providing training to the hotel employees, and then we have Best Western come in and provide training as well.

What other kinds of services does your hotel provide? Besides the room, we have concierge service through our front desk hotel staff, but not a specific concierge. We have a restaurant. We provide a hot breakfast buffet with an omelet station. We do wine tastings three nights a week. We have meeting rooms available and catering. We are a smaller hotel than probably some of these city properties. We get to know people, whereas at a bigger hotel, they don't know anybody. We definitely get to know our clients, and they appreciate it. It is nice to get to know them. We hear about their families, and all of that kind of stuff. We have grandparents who come here because their kids live here, and their kids have had babies, but now their grandkids are graduating high school—that is how long they have stayed here. So they have been with us for 18 to 20 years. Their families have grown up with us. The personal touch creates a value for them. How quickly can you build a relationship? It starts over the phone sometimes.

What areas does your hotel excel in servicing your guests? I would say in being very personable, when we talk about getting to know the people that are staying here. We get a lot of people that are only here for one night, and we do our best for them, but when they come back, that's when we really start to excel.

What do you think your hotel could do to improve? I think we do a pretty good job actually. We get pretty good Trip Advisor reviews, and really nice comments on Expedia and Google Plus, so I think we do a pretty good job, being a small hotel to service the guests that we have. We do okay. I think, if anything, it would be if we could be more consistent with it. Like when we are really busy, and there is only one person on; that is when we kind of lapse a little bit and don't score. If we could be more consistent to touch every person that same way, then we would be okay.

Give me an example of when you have received or provided outstanding service. That's why I brought this card from my guest. We get a lot of these, because we are around the corner from the hospital. We usually get three or four a year. This is actually a person who stayed here a couple of years before, but then two years after they stayed, they sent us a Christmas card. "Thinking of you this Christmas. Just wanted to thank you again for all that you did for me and my mom while my son was in the hospital. We are so truly blessed to have found such a caring group of professionals and your wonderful establishment. Thanks be to God, my son is home from the hospital and continuing to make progress in his recovery. We are so blessed. Wishing each of you and your families a very Merry Christmas. May 2014 bring you much peace, love, happiness, and good health. God bless." We get a bunch of these. We just had an older couple leave. She was only supposed to be here one day, but her husband came up from Danwood. Her husband was supposed to have a procedure, but the procedure kept getting postponed, so she had to continuously extend her stay. She could barely walk, and I think she needed a couple of procedures herself. She couldn't walk and couldn't breathe. They were thanking us profusely yesterday for everything that we did for them. You see people like that, and now, instead of her coming down to breakfast, we found out what she liked, and made her breakfast and took it up to her room.

Give me an example of when you have provided or received bad service. You know, we have definitely had people who thought we provided bad service. There is no question. You aren't going to please everybody. Whether we tried our best or not, it was just not good enough for them. Here is my personal experience. My wife and I had gone out to dinner, and it was at an Outback Steakhouse. We both ended up ordering the exact same item, but the portions came out so different, it was unbelievable. My wife had these huge portions of rice, salmon, and broccoli, and I got the smallest portions. It was an easy fix; we just traded. But the point was that the portions were not even close. And having been in the restaurant business, when two people order the exact same thing, the portions better come out exactly the same, or they have to be really, really close. So we called over the server, and he apologized and got us the manager. By the time they came over, we had finished our meal. But they didn't even offer us anything, which I thought for a chain restaurant was very odd. You would think they would offer you a free dessert or a free drink or coupons for next time, but we got nothing. I just thought that was weird. And we are both from the restaurant industry, so it is rare for us to say anything, but in this particular case, it was just so odd, because the portions were just so off. I don't know if the large portion was the correct portion, or if the small portion was the correct portion. But it was way off the mark. The point is to learn from the mistake, acknowledge it, and make an effort to correct it. If people see an effort, they are more forgiving.

Interview with Paul Dolce, General Manager of Dolce Hotel

What do you appreciate most from the vendors that provide services for you? I appreciate vendors that inform and communicate the same way that we communicate with our guests. We want them to communicate that their standards are for excellence, not for mediocre performance. When they communicate that, it is the first thing that we are looking for. It is to have a partner; whether they are doing dry cleaning or providing food or cleaning supplies, they match the standards we aim to achieve in our business. Communication is vital, whether we are talking about something positive or negative. So what we were just talking about, which was how we are doing here in this relationship coming up on our first year anniversary, I believe it is important that we have open and honest dialogue so that we can improve for each other. It has to be a partnership; it can't always be this person's fault or never that person's fault. This has to be a collaboration with both parties trying to help.

Now sometimes our customers will blame us for everything, and they will never take any responsibility; and unfortunately, that is the deal with customer service. They are the customer, and they are always right. So I like having open dialogue. I like having people who will respond quickly when I ask a question, either by email or a phone call. I expect a phone call within 24 hours, because everybody is busy, and everybody has to respect each other's time.

What areas do you think vendors can improve in general, and dry cleaning in particular? If a vendor provides bad service, then it will come back to your guests. That's right, because it is a reflection of you with every vendor that you do business with. The guests think of it as Dolce, Basking Ridge. They don't think of it as, "Okay, it's not Dolce, Basking Ridge; it's Sisko Foods, so it is okay." Or "It's Dolce, Basking Ridge, but it's this dry cleaning company, so it is okay." It is us, and that is why it is important that we have a partnership with the right vendors who match our standard of quality.

What we talked about, making sure that the communication is accurate with the expectations, that's why I asked you to clarify for me what the expectations are that you have, and that we have, and make sure that it matches for guest dry cleaning and employee dry cleaning. So, what I have been hearing, which I mentioned to you, were issues with the employee uniforms not being returned on a timely basis. So now that I understand your expectations, I want to make sure that is what my team's understanding is; and you are going to do the same thing on your end, and double check with your team.

How often do you meet with these vendors? As the general manager, I don't meet with them that often—maybe once a year. But what I ask is for all the department heads that are working with the vendors, to meet with them at least every quarter. But it depends on the vendor. With our food vendors that are making deliveries every week, we should be having dialogue with them on a regular basis. So I think, depending on who your primary contact is, on our end of it with the contact on the vendor's side, I always believe in staying in contact, even if it is just for a five-minute update on how things are going. You shouldn't always complain. You should also bring out the good things too. I am a firm believer that you have to reward positive behavior. So we try to recognize all the positive comments that we receive, so you are not, as a leader, always bringing up the negative ones. Bring up the positive ones, in addition to the negative ones, and you are being fair. So many leaders make the mistake of only communicating when there is a problem. And people don't respect that, because all they are going to do is wait to hear about a mistake. That, in my opinion, is not a good way to build a team.

Is Airbnb hurting your business now, and what do you see happening 10 years down the road? Well, the Airbnb statistics are pretty substantial. They have built a very successful business so far, and it would appear that they have plenty of room to grow. We haven't felt a dip in our business because of Airbnb. So we believe that right now in this market, for this property, we are not being affected by it. But I think our industry needs to pay very close attention to it. It is a business that has quite a bit of appeal to a lot of the general public. As they continue to grow, that is obviously going to equate to lost occupancy for hotels, because these people are now choosing these other sources instead of hotels. We can't ignore the trend of the public, and we need to adjust in our product.

If money and resources were not an issue, how would you improve service to your guests? Well, if money wasn't an issue, we would put refrigerators in every room. Right now, we just have them in the suites. We would lower prices in the restaurant and for room service. We would let people check out whatever time they wanted. Those are things that guests would find very appealing, if money wasn't an issue. Obviously, we have to try to manage our financial responsibility with the guests' expectations.

Do you receive any training from your management company or from the brand on how to handle clothes? Not in relation to clothes. What we are getting, as part of Wyndham Worldwide, is training from them in relation to PCI compliance, for computers and data from our guests, safety training, legal training, and sexual harassment training. There is a lot of human resources focused training, and a lot of general training, that can be delivered from a corporate standpoint, which we used to do from a Dolce corporate office, but now we are part of the Wyndham Worldwide Corporate instead. Then there is more specific training that still has to be done at the property level, which we cannot get from a corporate based program.

What other kinds of services does your hotel provide? Well, we provide an experience overall. The service provided is an experience. People come here for meetings, and they can come here for a meeting just for the day or for multiple days. So they are getting a guest room experience and a meeting experience, and obviously they are getting meals and having coffee breaks. Then to other guests, we are just a hotel, because maybe they are doing business with Verizon across the street. So we are just being used for the guest room, and possibly breakfast and dinner.

Sometimes we are used as a catering hall, and we host weddings. We have also been used for religious retreats, so we offer a lot of services. We have a lot of different types of business that we offer at this property, so we offer a wide variety of services as a result. But mostly, they relate to the meeting environment, the hotel environment, and the food and beverage environment.

What do you think your hotel could improve on in servicing your guests? One thing we have been hearing about is that we repainted and put new carpet in all the guest rooms, but we did not replace any of the desks or chairs or dressers in the rooms. Those are starting to show wear and tear. So that is an area where we can improve, by replacing all the furniture in our guest rooms.

Give me an example of when you have received or provided outstanding service. Well, we are ranked number one on Trip Advisor among our competitors in the area, which we are very proud of. We just had a review that I read online yesterday, which said that this place was the best place they had ever come to for a meeting. "The staff was extremely friendly," which was something that I was most proud of, because the first thing in hospitality is to be welcoming and friendly to the guest before you do anything else. This guest said that we did everything that we try to deliver, and it was done with pride every single day. This person said that it was better than they had ever seen, from being friendly to providing great service. They were missing something they were supposed to have delivered, and the person in purchasing went and found it in the storeroom for them. So they were very impressed with the follow-up. The food was some of the best food they had ever had at a hotel. It was a fantastic review, and it made us very proud.

Give me an example of when you have provided or received bad service. We do make mistakes, but you always have to try and learn. We had a guest tell us the other day that the shuttle that we have was supposed to be available to take them to a wedding, even if they missed the pickup time, and that we would have a shuttle on standby for them, but that was not correct. The guest had received misinformation, and we had to correct that for the guest. We only have two vans and a certain number of employees, so we have to schedule it when we have a wedding on the weekend. There can be a shuttle going every 30 minutes, but people attending these weddings can't just show up whenever they want to. They must sign up for one of these shuttles. But this guest was very upset with us, because they showed up late and expected a shuttle to be waiting. They were told it was fine if you show up late, and we had no shuttle and no bellman to drive them to the wedding. They were very upset with us, because their expectation was that we were going to be able to do that. They left very disappointed. The message for us is how critical communication is, and accurate communication, so that the guest shows up with the right expectation.

Now sometimes the guest is going to make something up, and there is nothing you can do about that. But we have to take the responsibility of making sure that we communicate accurately, so the guests have the proper expectation that we then can deliver on. Even if we make a mistake sometimes, we have to learn to overcome it.

Testimonials

"The Grand Summit Hotel has been utilizing Zak Kogan of GoGreen Organic Cleaners since May 2015. Since implementation, the hotel has received positive feedback from our clients and employees that utilize the service. The quality and attention to detail from GoGreen is second to none. Furthermore, GoGreen's tracking systems, accounting, billing, pick-up and delivery are flawless. They are the only cleaner that provides staff training for hotels in order to insure 100% guest satisfaction. We are very satisfied and recommend them without reservation..." – **Mark Giangiulio, General Manager, The Grand Summit Hotel**

"Zak Kogan of GoGreen Organic Cleaners has been a terrific addition to our vendor list. He and his company's attention to detail in regard to guest service, laundry, and valet, as well as the importance of professionalism in an upscale hotel, have become instrumental in helping us achieve a new level of Valet Cleaning Services offered to our guests and staff." – **Ed Reagoso, General Manager and Ownership Member, The Wilshire Grand Hotel**

"Zak is an extremely dependable individual, who prides himself on his consistency and organization. Additionally, he is the only dry-cleaning company I've ever worked with that provides staff training for the hotels to ensure guest satisfaction. I would happily recommend Zak and his team to any and all hotels looking for a reputable dry-cleaning service." – **Max Neufeld, Executive Housekeeper, Hyatt Morristown at Headquarters Plaza**

"Zak quickly gained my trust with his accountability and dedication to customer service. No job is too big or too small for his team. From billing to the delivery process, they are really organized and efficient." – **David Ruas, Hotel Manager, The Hampton Inn by Hilton Madison Square Garden**

"We had the pleasure of working directly with Zak Kogan and his company for the last four years. Their customer service and quality were always at the highest standards." – **Matthew Heymann, Director of Housekeeping, Sheraton Parsippany Hotel**

"Zak is very resourceful and consistent, and has gone above and beyond with use of his sub-divisions, outside of just dry cleaning. Zak has been providing us with his services since 09/2012. Zak and his team is the type of company you can always rely on to give 100%." – **Michael Priore, General Manager, Holiday Inn & Suites Parsippany**

About the Author

Zak Kogan is an entrepreneur, author, physicist and programmer, who built his career out of creating systems for a variety of industries, from clothing brands to hotels. He is inspired to provide outstanding service to all his clients, and he wants to teach others how to provide that same service in their own industries.

He was born in 1951, in the former Soviet Union, in the country which is now called Ukraine. Zak graduated from one of the top Soviet Union universities, with degrees in physics and computer science. In 1974, he opened his first clothing business. Zak immigrated to the United States in 1989, with his wife, two kids, and couple of suitcases, but he didn't speak the language, and had no money. Zak started out working as a consultant and programmer in the apparel business. In 1995, he opened a software company called Business Management Systems, which created one of the best product development systems at the time. It was implemented in several top apparel companies, including Donna Karan, Elie Tahari, and Theory, just to name a few. In 2007, Zak bought a dry cleaning company with the idea of developing a pick-up and delivery system, which would help busy people to save some time and money. In 2008, he started to work with major hotels, and created a system that allows for tracking guests' and employees' orders from the moment they are picked up from the hotel, to the dry cleaning facility, and back to the hotel. This system has been implemented with great success in multiple hotels in NY and NJ.

**Visit Zak Kogan's website:
GoGreenOrganicCleaners.com**

www.ingramcontent.com/pod-product-compliance
Lightning Source LLC
Chambersburg PA
CBHW060854220526
45466CB00003B/1374